The Periodic Table Series

Periodically, we're all geeks about the things we love and the Periodic Table Series has been created to celebrate this universal fact.

Inspired by The Periodic Table of Chemical Elements*, our experts have applied scientific logic to an eclectic range of subjects that regularly baffle beginners and fire-up fans. The outcome of this experiment is the essential guide you hold in your hand.

Geeky? Absolutely.
Hugely satisfying? Categorically.

*The Periodic Table of Chemical Elements orders all the known matter that makes up our world, from hydrogen to helium, by chemical properties and behaviour to give scientists a handy overview of a rather complex subject.

THE PERIODIC TABLE OF
FOOTBALL

NICK HOLT

EBURY
PRESS

10 9 8 7 6 5 4 3 2 1

Ebury Press, an imprint of Ebury Publishing,
20 Vauxhall Bridge Road,
London SW1V 2SA

Ebury Press is part of the Penguin Random House
group of companies whose addresses can be found
at global.penguinrandomhouse.com

Penguin
Random House
UK

First published by Ebury Press in 2016

www.eburypublishing.co.uk

A CIP catalogue record for this book is available
from the British Library

ISBN: 9781785031816

Printed and bound in China by Toppan Leefung

Penguin Random House is committed to a
sustainable future for our business, our readers
and our planet. This book is made from Forest
Stewardship Council® certified paper.

MIX
Paper from
responsible sources
FSC® C018179

Contents

The Periodic Table of
FOOTBALL

1 10 **Pe** Pelé								
2 9 **Ds** Di Stéfano								
3 13 **Eu** Eusébio								
4 6 **Mr** Moore							33 – **Sb** Sebes	38 – **Me** Meisl
5 4 **Bc** Beckenbauer	9 1 **Za** Zamora	13 4 **An** Andrade	17 5 **Mo** Monti	21 2/3 **S** Santos	25 7 **Mw** Matthews	29 4 **Bl** Blanchflower	34 2 **Rm** Ramsey	39 – **Bb** Busby
6 14 **Cf** Cruyff	10 11 **Zg** Zagallo	14 5/9 **Jc** Charles	18 3 **Fc** Facchetti	22 6 **Ed** Edwards	26 9 **Ct** Charlton	30 10 **Wa** Walter	35 – **Sk** Shankly	40 – **Js** Stein
7 10 **Pl** Platini	11 1 **Ya** Yashin	15 1 **Bn** Banks	19 6 **Ge** Gentile	23 6 **Am** Adams	27 1 **Sn** Shilton	31 9 **Mi** Milla	36 – **Mv** Milutinović	41 9 **Cl** Clough
8 10 **Ms** Messi	12 4 **Gl** Gullit	16 1 **Ne** Neuer	20 3 **Lu** Lúcio	24 16 **Lh** Lahm	28 11 **Gg** Giggs	32 3 **Md** Maldini	37 – **Fg** Ferguson	42 4 **Gu** Guardiola

POLYMORPHS

| 93   – **Ak** Alcock | 94   3 **Cm** Compton | 95   8 **So** Sócrates |

TRACE ELEMENTS

| 101   11 **Sh** Shackleton | 102   10 **St** Streltsov | 103   9 **Al** Albert |

ELEMENT KEY
TOP LEFT: ELEMENT NUMBER
TOP RIGHT: FAVOURITE SHIRT NUMBER

85 – **Bt** Blatter				

71 9 **Le** Leônidas	78 9 **Si** Sindelar	86 – **Hv** Havelange

59 6 **Wr** Wright	65 1 **Fk** Foulke	72 10 **Ps** Puskás	79 7 **Ga** Garrincha	87 – **He** Herrera

60 7 **Jz** Jairzinho	66 7 **Ra** Rahn	73 13 **Ft** Fontaine	80 7 **Be** Best	88 5/10 **Rt** Rattin

43 8 **Mz** Meazza	47 10 **Sf** Schiaffino	51 – **Ch** Chapman	55 – **Rt** Rimet	61 10 **Km** Kempes	67 6 **Bx** Baxter	74 13 **Gm** Müller	81 19 **Gz** Gascoigne	89 20 **Ro** Rossi
44 10 **Li** Liedholm	48 8 **Mh** Mühren	52 – **Mc** Michels	56 – **Hi** Hill	62 10 **Mt** Matthäus	68 8 **Sc** Schuster	75 10 **Ma** Maradona	82 7 **Ca** Cantona	90 10 **Ln** Lentini
45 1 **Sm** Schmeichel	49 10 **La** Laudrup	53 – **Lb** Lobanovskyi	57 – **Bs** Bosman	63 3 **Rc** Carlos	69 10 **Bg** Baggio	76 9 **Ro** Ronaldo	83 16 **Ke** Keane	91 – **Mu** Murdoch
46 6 **Xi** Xavi	50 10 **Bk** Bergkamp	54 – **Wg** Wenger	58 – **Av** Abramovich	64 8 **Gr** Gerrard	70 8/10 **Sv** Stoichkov	77 7 **Cr** Cr Ronaldo	84 10 **Zd** Zidane	92 7/9 **Su** Suárez

96 9/14 **We** Weah	97 4 **Jn** Jones	98 1 **Hg** Higuita	99 1 **Cv** Chilavert	100 7 **Bx** Beckham
104 8 **Hu** Hudson	105 10 **Cu** Cubillas	106 4 **Bg** Bergsson	107 7 **Lt** Le Tissier	108 10 **Rq** Riquelme

Introduction

Football is like chemistry. No, no, hear me out. Chemistry is a science, and the laws of science help explain the way the different elements of our universe hang together. For all the apparent randomness and unpredictability of human behaviour, we follow the laws of science and nature. Just as elements combine in chemistry to produce different and exciting results, so the disparate elements in football sometimes combine to produce something out of the ordinary.

In this book are the key elements of football, the players and managers, grouped according to the characteristics they bring to the game. Some elements are here by dint of exerting control over the way the game is policed and played. Some are elements that shine brightly and illuminate the game; some of these burn a little too brightly and extinguish themselves, so we only briefly see their full brilliance. Others have more subtle skills, they are catalysts and conductors, whose contribution is to bring out the best in those around them. There is praise too, for some of those rugged elements whose unpretentious skills are less admired, but no less important.

Having assessed all the factors that make up a player and designate his place in the pantheon we arrived at fourteen lab-tested groups in which to place our footballing elements: Precious Metals; Bedrocks; Solids; Sustainables; Conductors; Catalysts; Transmuters;

Porous; Unpredictables; Explosives; Combustibles; Corrosives and two 'rare earth' categories, Polymorphs and Trace Elements. Yes, this is sports science taken to the nth degree.

Most players could easily fit in three or four different sections, so we have looked for some kinship with the other components in a group or, in some instances, just followed a gut feeling that they belong in a particular group.

Many of these players may have finished their careers before the majority of this book's readers were born. If we believe what we read in the papers today the current scene is littered with glittering superstars. Totti, Ibrahimović, Tévez, Robben are all really good players, but none of them true greats, and none of them offering a new perspective on the game or the way it is played and coached. It is probably true to say that a career can only properly be assessed when it is over, the dust has settled and we can reflect on the true contribution of that career. That said, you'll find two contemporary greats listed – Lionel Messi and Cristiano Ronaldo would be world-class players in any era.

Some elements in the table might surprise you but they are here because their character or involvement in a specific event demands that we discuss them in the same breath as greater players. And a few are here because we are acknowledging what might have been, had circumstances been ever so slightly more in their favour.

There is no attempt to give a detailed biography of each player; all we've given is a name with a country of birth and a role in the game in brackets; this is more of a flavour, a feeling for the essence of a player, sometimes with a key moment that encapsulated that essence.

This is football's periodic table. Grasp this and you will have a feel for the checks and balances of the beautiful game.

Precious Metals

We begin with those priceless elements, the Precious Metals: the ones over which wars are fought and vast amounts of money change hands.

These are the stars in the footballing firmament, the jewels in the crown. They are players who are worshipped in some quarters, loved in most and respected even where they left heartbreak and loss. Add any of these players to an already very good team and you have potential world champions.

Column 1

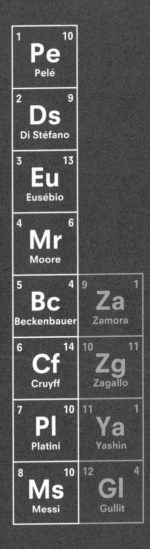

1 10 **Pe** Pelé	
2 9 **Ds** Di Stéfano	
3 13 **Eu** Eusébio	
4 6 **Mr** Moore	
5 4 **Bc** Beckenbauer	9 1 **Za** Zamora
6 14 **Cf** Cruyff	10 11 **Zg** Zagallo
7 10 **Pl** Platini	11 1 **Ya** Yashin
8 10 **Ms** Messi	12 4 **Gl** Gullit

1	10
Pe	
Pelé	

PELÉ

(Brazil, Genius)

Quite simply, Edson Arantes do Nascimento – Pelé as he is more commonly known – is the best player the game has ever seen. Modern pundits might claim this title for Lionel Messi, and Messi's accomplishments for Barcelona in Spain and in the Champions League are very special, but to be considered the greatest player the game has seen, surely a footballer must make a similar impact at international level?

Pelé first won the World Cup with Brazil as an exciting and flamboyant teenage prodigy in 1958. In 1962, Brazil won it again though Pelé missed most of the tournament through injury while, in 1966, the opposition were merciless and an underperforming side let him down. It wasn't until the 1970 tournament, now positioned as a wily playmaker behind a resourceful centre forward (Tostão), that Pelé showed his true genius. His range of passing and vision during that tournament were exceptional, and he still retained much of the power and aerial spring of his youth. He looked exactly what he was – the complete footballer.

Not only was Pelé a great player and athlete but he did it all with graciousness and charm. He never complained when he was targeted by the hard men; he just picked himself up and got on with it. (And usually got his revenge in the best way, by scoring, and winning).

Seventy-seven goals in ninety-two matches for Brazil was some record for a player who was never truly a natural striker. Pelé wore the number-ten shirt in all those games and he became indelibly associated with that number – commentators first started talking about the 'No.10' position in reference to Pelé's role just behind the centre forward. Others have filled the shirt with enormous distinction and craft but Pelé will always be THE number ten. Come on, Lionel, step up in 2018, you've only got one more chance …

There is one thing he isn't good at – punditry. If Pelé rates your team's chances, don't bother watching: this is the man who predicted, among others, Colombia would win the 1994 World Cup (they finished bottom of their first-round group).

ALFREDO DI STÉFANO

(Argentina, Forward)

For a while, a brief while in the early 1950s, Millonarios of Bogotá in Colombia could lay reasonable claim to be the strongest club side in the world. Not that they had many Colombians in the side. Most of the team were Argentinian exiles playing abroad because of a long-running footballers' strike in their home country. Among them was Alfredo Di Stéfano, a young Argentinian international; with Di Stéfano and Adolfo Pedernera playing inside forward, Millonarios had flair in abundance.

The success of the Colombian club attracted European scouts: Real Madrid liked what they saw and lured Di Stéfano to Europe. Two years after he arrived, the European Cup was played for the first time and Real Madrid dominated the early years: they won the first five finals, with Di Stéfano playing and scoring in every one. In 1958, Real won 3-2 against a Milan side containing Nils Liedholm, the Argentinian Grillo and the legendary Uruguayan centre forward Schiaffino. In 1960, Di Stéfano scored a hat-trick in the 7-3 mauling of Eintracht Frankfurt at Hampden Park (though he was more than matched by Ferenc Puskás, who scored four).

Argentina declined to enter the World Cup in 1950 and 1954, and Di Stéfano was persuaded to take Spanish nationality in 1956. A dropped point against Switzerland cost Spain its qualification for the 1958 tournament (Scotland won the group) and although Di Stéfano, now thirty-seven and apparently injured, was named in Spain's squad for Chile in 1962 he failed to make an appearance.

Rather oddly, the dual international made a handful of appearances as a 'guest' for Colombia in 1962.

Di Stéfano was a complete player – Bobby Charlton rates him as the best he saw. Operating as an inside forward or a deep-lying centre forward he had strength, balance and stamina to go with his silky South American skills and tricks – and he was a deadly finisher.

Di Stéfano is often cited as the best player never to play in a World Cup. He heads a small but illustrious group of such players never to grace the tournament: Adolfo Pedernera, Eduard Streltsov, George Best, Abedi Pele, Jari Litmanen, George Weah and Ryan Giggs also spring to mind, as well as one or two whose absence was self-imposed, like Eric Cantona and Bernd Schuster. One or two were denied for more tragic reasons, like the ill-fated Duncan Edwards and Valentino Mazzola.

EUSÉBIO

(Portugal, Forward)

It was well into the twentieth century before an African footballer imposed himself on the world game. That player was Portugal's brilliant striker, Eusébio.

At the 1966 World Cup Finals, the pre-tournament favourites were hosts England, holders Brazil and the fast-improving West German team. No one gave Portugal much of a chance: despite the presence of the talented Benfica forward line they were deemed unlikely to make it out of a group containing Brazil and a talented Hungarian side. As it transpired, Brazil were a disappointment while Portugal won all three of their games with ease.

The Portuguese star was Mozambique-born Eusébio, a striker of electrifying pace with a ferocious shot from either foot. After a quiet start he clicked in the third group game against Brazil, scoring twice to eliminate the holders and setting up a quarter-final against the tournament's surprise package, North Korea.

A complacent Portugal found themselves 3-0 down before Eusébio provided some much needed inspiration. His pace and skill were too much for the Koreans, and he scored four times, including twice from the penalty spot.

After that, the semi-final proved something of a damp squib: Eusébio scored a consolation penalty to cement his place as the tournament's top scorer, but Portugal were defeated 2-1 by the eventual winners, England.

At club level, Eusébio won a stack of league titles as Benfica dominated at home, and played in four European Cup finals in the 1960s, though winning only the first, a 5-3 thriller against Real Madrid. Eusébio scored twice in a game which saw the young star line up against two great players at the other end of their journey: Alfredo Di Stéfano and Ferenc Puskás. Some treat for the fans.

Eusébio blazed a trail for black players: he made his Portugal debut in 1961, seventeen years before Viv Anderson, a Nottingham-born son of West Indian parents, made his debut for England.

BOBBY MOORE

(England, Defender)

Bobby Moore was the best defender ever to play the game, and that includes a bevy of fantastic Italian players. He was the epitome of calm – he was never hurried (just as well, he wasn't quick), never dived into tackles unless absolutely necessary, and was able to double as an attacking outlet with his ability to play an accurate, raking pass out of defence. His sangfroid was shown during one league match when the referee was poleaxed by the ball and knocked out cold: while everyone else flapped and dithered, Moore calmly picked up the ref's whistle and boomed for the game to stop so the official could receive treatment.

Towards the end of his international career, Moore's lack of pace let him down; it is entirely possible that were he playing now, he would be used as a holding midfield player in the Andrea Pirlo mould – indeed, he started his career as a half back in the fifties. But anyone who remembers his utter dominance at the 1966 World Cup and his immaculate display against Brazil in 1970 saw a very special player at the peak of his powers.

It was an odd quirk of the 1966 World Cup squad that the majority of them proved unsuitable for football management; only Jack Charlton of the eleven that started the final could be said to have been a success as a manager. Moore nearly took Southend United out of the league in the 1980s. Moore seemed ideal management material, but two iffy years at Southend in the bottom division suggested otherwise.

FRANZ BECKENBAUER

(West Germany, Defender/Midfielder/Manager)

Franz Beckenbauer is closely comparable with Moore, except Beckenbauer won more accolades because he played for his country's dominant club side. Beckenbauer started his career as a midfield player who could both win the ball and use it. His progression backwards to defender made perfect sense, such was his instinctive reading of the game and the quality of his interceptions. With uncompromising, old-fashioned defenders like Vogts and Schwarzenbeck around him, the West Germany defence was tough to penetrate: in 1974, Beckenbauer was integral to the country's World Cup victory.

Like his compatriot Gerd Müller, Beckenbauer quit international football at the top and went to earn his money playing in the US. His time there was the source of the fabulous (probably apocryphal) story of a wealthy but ignorant club grandee, insisting 'the Kraut get his ass forwards – we don't pay him the big bucks to sit in defence.' Erm... yes you do, and he is worth every penny.

Beckenbauer added a second World Cup win to his long list of achievements, this time as a manager in 1990 – a feat he shares with only Mário Zagallo.

Articulate, intelligent and an astute critic of the game, if Beckenbauer has a fault, it is an autocratic air and a degree of intolerance for those less able than himself. Since ending a second stint as caretaker manager at Bayern Munich, he has operated in a directorial capacity both at Bayern and for Germany's successful 2006 World Cup bid. He also has a profile as a pundit and newspaper columnist. He is a man used to winning, so when he expresses an opinion on German footballing issues, he tends to get his way.

Beckenbauer is often referred to as Der Kaiser – a reference both to his imperious displays and that touch of autocracy.

JOHAN CRUYFF

(Holland, Forward)

Johan Cruyff was a talented youth player who became a talented adult player who became a talented coach. He fits the bill for most of the groups in the book, but his genius demands a place in this section.

Cruyff was leader and the core of the greatest side Holland put on to the field (with all due respect to Gullit and company). He was a consistent and reliable performer; his tricks were so effective because he only tried them when the percentages were good. He won the Dutch league with Feyenoord when he was thirty-seven. He pulled the strings both for Ajax and Holland, he was at the heart of everything they did and achieved, and he managed Barcelona with the same passion and involvement. He changed Barcelona for good, instilling in the club as player and coach the attacking instinct and ball-retention skills that brought them such success.

No one expected him to retire from international football just before the 1978 World Cup, which he did after a kidnap threat while he was at Barcelona, and no one quite knew what to make of some of the bizarre philosophy he spouted.

When Cruyff got the ball you waited while he waited, your breath held, wondering what particular magic trick you were about to witness. He could be aggressive and cussed when he felt aggrieved. He has had spats with Marco van Basten and Louis van Gaal and was the first Dutch player to be sent off in an international match (for which he received a twelve-month ban).

Cruyff didn't do things the way everyone else did them, he did them the Cruyff way and he stuck to his guns. He was a genius so here he sits in Column 1 with the rest of the Precious Metals. The third best player ever to play the game.

'There's only one moment in which you can arrive in time. If you're not there, you're either too early or too late.'
Johan Cruyff

MICHEL PLATINI

(France, Attacking Midfielder)

France has had two great football sides. One was the 1998 World Cup winning team with Zidane and a great defence. The first had Michel Platini at the heart of a fantastic midfield foursome that made its mark in the 1984 European Cup and 1986 World Cup.

This four were known as the *carré magique* (magic square) and consisted of Platini, Alain Giresse, Jean Tigana and Luis Fernández. Fernández and Giresse played wider in the square, both capable of winning the ball and distributing it precisely and economically. Tigana was the runner and ball carrier possessed of seemingly endless stamina and athleticism. The *éminence grise* was Platini. Slightly stooped and unathletic in his gait, the French playmaker rarely seemed to achieve more speed than a gentle stroll unless it was to make a late surge into the box to get on the end of a cross. His passing was immaculate; he seemed to caress the ball rather than strike it, but it always ended up where he wanted it to be.

Platini's strike rate of forty-one goals in seventy-two international matches shames many strikers. He was a power in Europe by the start of the eighties but gained global acclaim with an excellent showing in the 1982 World Cup, during which an unlikely French team reached the semi-finals and lost in a thrilling game against West Germany – they were unfortunate to be facing eleven men after a horror tackle by the German goalkeeper, Toni Schumacher, went unpunished.

Better was to come in 1984 when Platini orchestrated a successful European Championship campaign on home soil. Seven goals in three group games (including successive hat-tricks, an astonishing statistic for a midfield player) were followed by a win in a cliff-hanger semi-final against Portugal. Defeating Spain in the final, France had its first major tournament victory.

At club level, Platini joined Juventus in 1982 and, after a difficult start, the investment paid off as the team won the European Cup as well as *Serie A*. Platini retired at thirty-two and began a career in football politics. He has proved as adept at that as he was at playing the game, and has been UEFA president since 2007. Generally, he has been a voice of reason and spoken for the good of the game, although the actions of his organisation have not always mirrored the positive words.

It is odd that France won their first two major championships (European in 1984, World Cup in 1998) without a striker worth the name. In 1984 their only striker of note, Dominique Rocheteau, was injured and didn't get through the tournament, so Platini's goals were a godsend. In 1998 the cupboard was bare – Jean-Pierre Papin and Eric Cantona had been and gone. By 2000 at the European Championship Arsène Wenger had provided the solution by converting winger Thierry Henry into a centre forward.

LIONEL MESSI

(Argentina, Winger/Forward)

Messi is the best player of the last decade and a quite brilliant dribbler and finisher. Like his countryman Diego Maradona, Messi is small and well-balanced, but surprisingly difficult to knock off the ball. Messi's achievements with Barcelona are astonishing – on the pitch, at least. With the Argentinian as their talisman Barça have won title after title in Spain and Europe and done it with panache and flair. With Messi in the side the endless possession has a purpose – get the ball to Lionel, he will score. He usually does.

Inexplicably, Messi's performances for Argentina have never matched those he produces with remarkable consistency for Barcelona and so many in Spain and Europe make claims for his place in the pantheon of greats more urgently than his fellow South Americans.

In the 2010 World Cup, the Argentinian team crashed out in the quarter-finals. In 2014, although Messi started that tournament well, his team laboured past Switzerland, beat a timid Belgium by one goal and needed penalties to defeat a Dutch side with a panicky defence in the knock-out rounds. Meeting Germany again, this time in the final, Argentina were beaten by a much superior side. Despite their loss, Messi won the Player of the Tournament award – although was seriously embarrassed by this. The most disappointing aspect of his play during both World Cups was the lack of visible leadership he offered his teammates – he never stopped trying, but there was none of the thrilling bravura he shows for Barcelona. With the clock ticking, Messi has one more chance for World Cup glory – he will be thirty-one during the 2018 tournament.

At time of writing Messi is about to play his 100th match for Argentina. He has forty-six goals in ninety-nine games, but only five in fifteen World Cup Finals matches, compared with his record of nine goals every ten games for Barcelona.

Bedrocks

These are football's bedrocks. These elements are a little less glamorous than the Precious Metals, but they are still at the core of the game, an essential part of its appeal. They are the indispensable ones: the first name on the team sheet, the prima donna players the coach turns to when one of the star players is having an off day.

Many of them were an inspiration for others in later generations, like José Andrade, others were at the heart of a golden era for their team, like Ruud Gullit and his cohorts. They are all, unquestionably, among the greats of the game.

Column 2

1 Pe **10** Pelé		
2 Ds **9** Di Stéfano		
3 Eu **13** Eusébio		
4 Mr **6** Moore		
5 Bc **4** Beckenbauer	**9** Za **1** Zamora	**13** An **4** Andrade
6 Cf **14** Cruyff	**10** Zg **11** Zagallo	**14** Jc **5/9** Charles
7 Pl **10** Platini	**11** Ya **1** Yashin	**15** Bn **1** Banks
8 Ms **10** Messi	**12** Gl **4** Gullit	**16** Ne **1** Neuer

9		1
	Za	
	Zamora	

RICARDO ZAMORA

(Spain, Goalkeeper)

Italy, England and Germany have all boasted great goalkeepers, but all have had spells when the cupboard seemed a little bare. Less so Spain. Ricardo Zamora was the best goalkeeper around the pre-war days and he was the first in a line of succession that has remained unbroken through Antoni Ramallets, José Iribar, Luis Arconada, Andoni Zubizarreta and Iker Casillas. All of these rate as world-class, but none better than the first, Zamora. Reports from the 1934 World Cup and friendly matches highlight his athleticism and strength – at six foot four he was especially tall for the 1920s. He was brave, too, carrying on to the end of a match against England despite suffering broken ribs early in the game. It was the game that saw England's unbeaten record against continental opposition broken.

Zamora liked a drink and was a chain smoker. He was a fashion icon, popularising the polo-neck goalkeeping sweater (a very sixties man-about-town long before the sixties). None of this high life seemed to diminish his ability between the sticks. During the political crisis in Spain, the war between Franco's fascists and the republican government, Zamora spent some time in prison and later sought refuge in France. But his role was somewhat equivocal – he was later awarded the medal of honour by Franco.

Zamora was initially a successful coach after he retired: he led Atlético Aviación (the club that later became Atlético Madrid) to their first *La Liga* title in 1939–40, and won a second the following year. He never quite matched that success again, though he carried on for another decade and was even, briefly, the coach of the Spanish international team.

The legacy lives on: just as Iker Casillas's powers appear to be waning Spain have unearthed another gem of a goalkeeper in Manchester United's David De Gea – who is being lured home by Real Madrid at the time of writing.

MÁRIO ZAGALLO

(Brazil, Wide Midfielder)

Mário Zagallo wore the number-eleven shirt for the 1958 Brazilian team. In the 1950s, No.11 meant an old-fashioned winger: a quick, skilful player whose job was to round the full back and ping over crosses for a centre forward. Zagallo was different; he was the prototype of the modern wide-midfield player.

After a dull start to the 1958 World Cup Finals tournament the Brazilian coach, Feola, made two key changes, bringing in the youngster Pelé and the maverick Garrincha. Garrincha was an out-and-out winger, a purely attacking player, so Zagallo on the other flank compensated by playing in a more withdrawn role, augmenting the midfield and helping out in defence when the opponents had the ball. This counterbalancing of the two wide players became a common tactic throughout the next decade. The Brazilian coach also had one of his half backs play very deep, effectively making a four-man defence. When Zagallo tucked into midfield in defensive posture, the Brazilians had, without doing anything too drastic, turned the old-fashioned WM formation into a modern 4-3-3. Amid all the brilliance and talent around him, it was Zagallo's intelligence, adaptability and work rate that helped make Brazil such a complete team.

That intelligence served Zagallo in good stead when he was appointed coach of the national team in 1970, just before the World Cup. He had the sense not to be over technical with a massively gifted side and, left to it, they won the tournament with some scintillating football. The centre forward, Tostão, hard-working and intelligent, played a selfless team role similar to Zagallo's own.

Zagallo was still on the scene twenty-four years later, when Brazil won the trophy again in 1994, working as a wise old head alongside coach Carlos Alberto Parreira, and he remains active in Brazilian football in his eighties.

Zagallo was the first man to both play in and later coach a World Cup winning team.

LEV YASHIN

(Ussr, Goalkeeper)

Lev Yashin or Gordon Banks? Gordon Banks or Lev Yashin? Trying to decide who was the best goalkeeper the game has seen to date, there was a hair's breadth between these two. Yashin had durability – but then he didn't have to cope with losing an eye. He made his debut in 1954, and was still in the Soviet squad at the 1970 World Cup, although he was third choice and selected more for his experience and coaching.

If World Cup performances are the yardstick then Banks was a rock for England in 1966 and spectacularly good four years later. Yashin was fantastic in his first tournament in 1958 and earned due plaudits for a brilliant display against Brazil (matched by Banks twelve years later, against the same opposition). In 1962, Yashin was less secure, making a couple of errors, including, unforgivably for a keeper of his class, conceding a goal direct from a corner. Nevertheless, he won the European Footballer of the Year award in 1963 after an outstanding season.

Yashin played his entire career for one club, Dynamo Moscow (he was born in the city). He won a number of titles in his home country, but got little chance to prove himself against continental opposition as the Soviets declined to put their champions forward for the European Cup until 1966–67 (fear of failure a defining theme of Soviet sport). By this time Dynamo Kiev had emerged as the strongest team in the Federation. Dynamo Moscow,

despite never dropping out of the top flight in either
the Soviet or subsequent Russian leagues, won the title
with Yashin in the side in 1963 and again in 1976, but have
failed to do so since.

Yashin was the subject of a poem by Yevgeny Yevtushenko
called 'Goalkeeper Coming Out of His Goal'. Yevtushenko
was one of the most significant poets of the Soviet era, and
had a rare ability to balance criticism of and compliance
with the regime.

RUUD GULLIT

12   4

Gl

Gullit

(Holland, Sweeper/Midfielder/Forward)

In the 1950s, AC Milan transformed their fortunes by
hiring the 'Gre-No-Li' trio of attacking players from
Sweden (Gunnar Gren, Gunnar Nordahl and Nils
Liedholm). In 1987 the club, not only used to success but
also one of the wealthiest in Europe after the takeover by
Silvio Berlusconi in 1986, repeated the tactic. This time,
they turned to Holland.

From Dutch champions PSV Eindhoven they bought
the talented and versatile Ruud Gullit. Used mainly as
a forward at PSV, Gullit was equally at home dropping
into midfield and even operated effectively as a *libero* or
sweeper on occasions. He was strong as an ox and quick
with it, good in the air and intelligent; a one-man epitome
of the Dutch 'Total Football' philosophy. As well as Gullit,
Milan bought two players from Ajax; Marco van Basten, a
sharpshooter, and Frank Rijkaard, a tough and disciplined
defensive midfielder.

Gullit was the leader: he dictated the patterns and
the tempo for Milan and Holland and loaded the gun. Van
Basten was the bullet, Rijkaard the insurance. Together
the three became known as the Holy Trinity.

Milan won *Serie A* and followed with successive
European Cup victories in 1989 and 1990. In the first of
these Milan destroyed Steaua Bucharest, two goals each

for van Basten and Gullit in a 4-0 win. A year later Rijkaard scored the game's only goal as Benfica were beaten.

Holland gained too. In 1988 they won the European Championship, beating the feared Germans in the semi-final and a terrific Soviet Union side in the final, with a Gullit header and a van Basten volley of fearsome power.

In the 1990 World Cup Rijkaard was sent off against Germany for spitting – and two years later van Basten was forced to retire at thirty-one. Rijkaard moved back to Ajax and Gullit moved to England to play for and manage Chelsea. He spoke the language better than the natives but never enjoyed the successful managerial career many expected.

It wasn't just about the Holy Trinity, as they became known. Milan had a back four of Tassotti, Costacurta, Baresi and Maldini, arguably the best club defence ever assembled.

Column 3

1   10
Pe
Pelé

2   9
Ds
Di Stéfano

3   13
Eu
Eusébio

4   6
Mr
Moore

5 4	9 1	13 4
Bc	**Za**	**An**
Beckenbauer	Zamora	Andrade

6 14	10 11	14 5/9
Cf	**Zg**	**Jc**
Cruyff	Zagallo	Charles

7 10	11 1	15 1
Pl	**Ya**	**Bn**
Platini	Yashin	Banks

8 10	12 4	16 1
Ms	**Gl**	**Ne**
Messi	Gullit	Neuer

13   4

An

Andrade

JOSÉ LEANDRO ANDRADE

(Uruguay, Half Back/Defensive Midfielder)

Looking at the pictures of the 1930 Uruguay World Cup winning team, you will see ten white or Latino guys, one black man. One of the few surviving photos of the squad shows the team in a café in Amsterdam – the black player is behind the bar, serving drinks, which pretty much sums up the prevalent prejudice. If you were black, you had to be a really *really* good player to be accepted into South American teams before the war (and for a good few years afterwards). Andrade was better than good; he was the heartbeat and the driving force of that first successful Uruguayan side.

In Uruguay they have a word, *garra*. It doesn't have a direct translation – the closest we have is 'bottle'. Andrade had the *garra*. During the 1930 World Cup tournament, the Argentinian playmaker and centre half, Luís Monti, intimidated opponents with his bulky presence, scowling demeanour and fierce tackling. But facing Argentina in the final, Uruguay were unbowed: their own enforcer, José Nasazzi, was strong at the back while Andrade and the Uruguay midfield simply outran the opposition in the second half, turning a 2-1 deficit into a 4-2 triumph.

Andrade didn't appear for the national team again after that, but in the victorious 1950 side there was another Andrade, Víctor Rodríguez Andrade, who adopted his uncle's name as a mark of respect. Guess what? He was the only black player in the team. Andrade senior died in poverty in his fifties.

Garra = fortitude + desire.

14   5/9

Jc

Charles

JOHN CHARLES

(Wales, Centre Half/Centre Forward)

The Gentle Giant. John Charles earned the first half of his epithet by way of his good nature and impeccable conduct on the field of play. In a twenty-three-year career there is no record of him being so much as booked for a rough tackle (although a rough tackle in the 1950s meant sawing someone's leg off at the knee) and Charles survived five years in the unforgiving environment of Italy's *Serie A* without retaliation.

He was also, as the second half of his epithet suggests, a big man. Charles was six-foot-two tall, with a broad chest and big, muscular legs. He was terrific in the air, had a powerful shot and was quicker than expected for someone of his stature. Born in Swansea, he was snapped up by Leeds United as a teenager and captained the Yorkshire side as they won promotion to the top flight. There was some debate as to whether Charles was better at centre forward or centre half, but this was no mere utility player: he was world class in either position.

Charles became the highest profile British footballing export to date when he transferred to Juventus in 1957 for more than double the previous record fee. The Italians loved him – he is still regarded by many Juve fans as their greatest ever centre forward. Sympathy must be felt for Wales, then, as they were deprived of their best player through injury for their most important game ever, at the 1958 World Cup, and still nearly held Brazil, losing 2-1 with a heroic display.

After his league career ended with a spell in his native country at Cardiff, Charles joined Hereford United and as player-manager he built the side that famously beat Newcastle in an FA Cup match in 1972 and won election to the Football League.

He is remembered chiefly for the then exorbitant £65,000 transfer fee, but that understates the man and the player – he was a world-class footballer of the very highest order.

Impassable at head height, and impervious to provocation.

15   1

Bn

Banks

GORDON BANKS

(England, Goalkeeper)

It may seem an odd thing to say, given their problems with the position in recent times, but England have had some fabulous goalkeepers over the years. From Gordon Banks in the 1960s through to the retirement of David Seaman, there was an unbroken line of high-quality goalkeepers, not unlike the thread Spain enjoyed (see Zamora above). Through the latter part of the 1970s there was a glut: excellent keepers like Phil Parkes and Joe Corrigan barely got a look in for England as the No.1 jersey swapped between Ray Clemence and Peter Shilton. Eventually, Shilton became the accepted main man and he kept the position throughout the eighties. Chris Woods and Seaman kept up the standard. Only after Seaman did the flakiness that has plagued England become the norm. There are signs, though, that Joe Hart is maintaining greater consistency and may take England back to the days of reliability.

Gordon Banks was a massive presence in the 1966 World Cup winning side and he was even better in 1970 when he made one of football's most memorable saves – from Pelé's header in a splendid group match. Two years later he was finished after losing the sight in one eye in a motor accident.

Banks was a confident and agile shot-stopper and a good organiser. Maybe he lacked Shilton or Schmeichel's presence coming off his line, but he more than made up for it with his elasticity and agility. He is a serious rival for Yashin's spot in an All-Time World XI.

Spare a thought, though, for Peter Bonetti. Thrown into action at the last moment for the 1970 World Cup quarter-final when Banks fell ill, Bonetti had a horror match and was reviled by England's fans. The fault lay with the management, who failed to give Bonetti more friendly appearances to build confidence – he was a terrific goalkeeper.

Within a year of winning the World Cup, Banks was dropped by his club, Leicester City. It transpired that they wanted to cash in the thirty-year-old and blood their hot new prospect, a teenager by the name of Peter Shilton...

MANUEL NEUER

(Germany, Goalkeeper)

The best goalkeeper of the modern era is still only twenty-nine at time of writing. Better than Schmeichel, Buffon, Casillas, Barthez and Cech? Yes.

The modern goalkeeper has to do a bit more to contribute to the team. I don't mean they should all take free kicks like José Chilavert – the Paraguayan international who scored sixty-two times during his career – but they need to be the first spark in the attack as well as the last line of defence. In these days of statistics, the goalkeeper has his pass completion, the accuracy of his kicks from hand and throwing distances all measured, as well as his ability to stop the ball going in the net (although if he isn't very good at the stopping bit, the rest of it becomes irrelevant).

All goalkeepers are different: some catch crosses, some punch them away; some are quick off the line, others prefer not to risk being rounded; some like a big wall at set pieces, others prefer to get a view of the kicker. Neuer's great strength is his decision-making; he seems to know when to come and catch a cross and when to let his defenders deal with it. He is alert to danger and consequently always seems to be in the right position to make the save. Coming off his line, he is simply sensational. Neuer works hard on his speed over the ground (like most modern goalkeepers, he is a big unit) so he can operate almost as a sweeper for both Bayern Munich and the German side. Both teams play a high defensive line, knowing that behind them is a man with both great anticipation and the courage to back his excellent judgement. Manuel Neuer has almost a full set of titles; he was a significant factor in Germany's World Cup victory in 2012, has won *Bundesliga*, Champions League and Club World Cup titles with Bayern Munich, and is a stalwart of the annual UEFA and FIFA teams of the year. When Neuer retires he may be acclaimed as the best ever in his position.

Neuer was only third choice for Germany until 2009, when the tragic death of Robert Enke made him second in line. When René Adler was injured before the 2010 World Cup, Neuer had his big chance. He seized it with both gloved hands.

Solids

It is absolutely no use having a glittering array of attacking talent and no defence: you just end up with the late 1990s Newcastle team. Every team needs Solids for balance. And balance is the essence of a good side. Messi, Suárez and Neymar would be far less potent if they had nothing behind them – Busquets and Piqué are an equally integral part of Barça's success; they just get less column inches because they don't have the licence to display flair that their colleagues enjoy. Even Precious Metals need a few Solids around them – it shows their lustre to better effect.

Most of these players, by the nature of the category, are defenders. But the group needn't exclude those further forward on the pitch: Emile Heskey or the above-named Sergio Busquets, so too Claude Makélélé or James Milner.

Column 4

13 4 **An** Andrade	17 5 **Mo** Monti	21 2/3 **S** Santos
14 5/9 **Jc** Charles	18 3 **Fc** Facchetti	22 6 **Ed** Edwards
15 1 **Bn** Banks	19 6 **Ge** Gentile	23 6 **Am** Adams
16 1 **Ne** Neuer	20 3 **Lu** Lúcio	24 16 **Lh** Lahm

17	5
Mo	
Monti	

LUIS MONTI

(Argentina, Centre Half)

Solids don't come much more solid than this footballer, who was nearly as wide as he was tall. Back in the day (the pre-war years) when most footballers were pretty hard, Luis Monti stood out. He could dominate a game through sheer presence and reputation.

Monti was the key player for Argentina as they breezed through the early rounds of the inaugural World Cup in 1930. In the final, Monti was widely expected to negate the Uruguayans but inspired by their bedrock, Andrade, they were less easily cowed, and won 4-2.

Four years later and Monti was back in another World Cup final against Czechoslovakia – but this time he played for Italy. This might seem unusual, but playing for two countries was common in the years either side of the war. If a South American player came to Europe, he would generally be adopted by his host country: Enrique Guaita and Raimundo Orsi, Italy's wingers in the 1934 final, were both, like Monti, born in Argentina and won caps for Argentina before crossing the Atlantic. Such players were known as the *oriundi* (loosely, the immigrants) and even in the 1950s the process was a common one: big-name players like Di Stéfano, José Santamaría and Omar Sívori all appeared for two different countries.

Monti enjoyed better luck in his second World Cup final. This time, he had Giuseppe Meazza ahead of him to carry the bulk of the creative load so Monti could concentrate on terrorising the Czech forward line. It took Italy extra time to win the competition but Angelo Schiavio's goal settled it. Odd circumstances, but the game had its first dual World Cup finalist – he was eclipsed by Meazza and Giovanni Ferrari four years later as Italy won in Paris.

Monti's luck ran out later in the year when he broke his foot in the second minute of a friendly against England, to supposedly decide the world's best team (England hadn't entered the World Cup). The match turned sour – it became known as 'The Battle of Highbury' – with the

Italians believing the tackle on Monti was a deliberate ploy from Ted Drake. In the days before substitutes, they had to play almost the entire game with ten men and there were numerous walking wounded by the end of the match. England won 3-2, for what it was worth.

Solidity rating: impossible to pass and keep both legs.

GIACINTO FACCHETTI

(Italy, Left Back)

Helenio Herrera's famous Inter Milan side of the 1960s were best known for their *catenaccio* system of defending (see Corrosives), but their counter-attacking threat was a vital component of their style of play as well. It helped that they had Giacinto Facchetti, one of the great counter-attacking full backs and a player that changed general perceptions about defenders.

Facchetti was very tall for a full back, over six foot three and very quick, which helped him recover if the team lost possession. If he couldn't, the left-sided central defender would be there waiting to help.

Facchetti didn't just have pace, but also used the ball well; his passing and crossing were as good as most wingers. He contributed goals, too – he once scored ten in a season as he won his third *Serie A* title in 1965–6. He finished his career with four *Series A* wins, two European Cups and a European Championship medal. He also played in the 1970 World Cup as captain of Italy although there were beaten in the final by the best Brazilian side ever seen.

Facchetti could equally appear in the Catalysts section; the idea of the full back who had freedom to attack but was sound in defence as well was relatively new, and he was the first truly great exponent of the position now known as a wing back. In later years at club level he looked almost equally accomplished playing as a sweeper. The ninety-four caps he won for his country was a long-standing record, until broken by Dino Zoff.

Facchetti died in 2006 after forty-six years with Inter Milan, latterly as an ambassador and president. There is no longer a No.3 in the Inter squad.

Solidity rating: no passing on the outside. Wait until he's gone and try and sneak through.

CLAUDIO GENTILE

(Italy, Defender/Man-Marker)

If Italian defenders have always been known for stretching the rules to the limit, then Claudio Gentile was the nonpareil of the dirty-tricks brigade. A little shirt-pull here, a little rake of the leg there, maybe a crafty tug of the hair, Gentile may have run his studs down his own mother's leg if he was told to mark her. He even looked like a hit-man for the Cosa Nostra, especially with the moustache he sported in 1982.

At the 1982 World Cup, defending champions Argentina were heavily reliant on their young tyro, Diego Maradona. They lost their opening match but qualified for the second phase and their reward was a mini group against Italy and Brazil.

So unforgiving was Maradona's encounter with Gentile, it was a miracle he didn't get sent off for retaliation.

The game was billed as 'Beauty v. The Beast': Brazil's myriad talents against Italy's formidable defence, including Gaetano Scirea and Antonio Cabrini. But it was Gentile's day. Booked after thirteen minutes he was forced to defend conventionally and he did so with great aplomb, extinguishing the threat of the masterful Zico. Italy defended superbly, while at the other end Paolo Rossi took three of the four chances that came his way. Italy won 3-2 and went on to win the tournament.

Gentile won a handful of *Serie A* titles as well as the World Cup, all with his main club, Juventus – no wonder, perhaps, seeing as they boasted Gentile, Scirea and

Cabrini in front of goalkeeper Dino Zoff, the brilliant Marco Tardelli in front of them in midfield and Rossi up front.

Solidity rating: unshakeable, but inclined to induce precipitation in others, mainly tears and night sweats.

LÚCIO

(Brazil, Centre Half)

One of the most underrated defenders of the modern era. With his three main clubs in Europe Lúcio has played in two Champions League finals (winning one with Inter Milan, losing with Leverkusen), won three *Bundesliga* titles (with Bayern Munich) and a *Serie A* title (Mourinho's Inter again). While at Leverkusen he won the World Cup with Brazil, and played in two more in 2006 and 2010. A CV isn't everything, but this one is pretty good.

England fans may remember Lúcio for a mistake in Michael Owen's goal against Brazil in the 2002 World Cup, but this was a rare blemish. Here's another more telling statistic: he once played four consecutive games without committing a foul. Why is this so significant? Because the modern game is stacked against defenders. Attackers are given much more protection than used to be the case and tackles that once would have been applauded now earn yellow and even red cards. The art is to time the tackle, or better still avoid it by reading the game and making an interception – and most importantly, to stay on your feet. Lúcio was terrific at this waiting game: his carriage and technique were similar to Rio Ferdinand. This was why he rarely gave away free kicks or penalties.

Lúcio is still playing for FC Goa in the Indian Super League at the time of writing, but it is his fantastic displays in the World Cup, the Champions League and across Europe that set him apart from most of his contemporaries.

Solidity rating: unlikely to collapse in a heap, so best go around.

Column 5

17 5 **Mo** Monti	**21** 2/3 **S** Santos	**25** 7 **Mw** Matthews
18 3 **Fc** Facchetti	**22** 6 **Ed** Edwards	**26** 9 **Ct** Charlton
19 6 **Ge** Gentile	**23** 6 **Am** Adams	**27** 1 **Sn** Shilton
20 3 **Lu** Lúcio	**24** 16 **Lh** Lahm	**28** 11 **Gg** Giggs

21	2/3
S	
Santos	

DJALMA SANTOS AND NÍLTON SANTOS

(Brazil, Both Full Backs)

Brazil were a brilliant side in 1958 and 1962, with a parade of fantastic attacking players. Early Brazilian sides were known for this, but the class of '58 had something new – a top-class goalkeeper, Gilmar, equally exceptional defenders and two of the finest full backs ever to play the game.

Djalma and Nílton Santos were no relation, despite what some lazy journalists wrote at the time. They also had very different playing styles but there was a clear parallel between their careers.

Nílton was four years the elder and made his Brazil debut in 1949, Djalma three years later. Neither covered themselves in glory at the 1954 World Cup. During the tempestuous quarter-final between Brazil and Hungary known as The Battle of Berne, Nílton was dismissed for fighting with József Bozsik, the Hungarian captain (it was uncharacteristic of both men and indicative of the heated nature of that game). Djalma was luckier – he should also have gone for chasing Zoltán Czibor up the touchline.

A 4-2 defeat by England in 1956 (including a rare roasting for Nílton by the recalled Stanley Matthews) led to a change of tactic by the Brazilian manager, Feola. He adopted a new four-man defence, and it suited Nílton Santos in particular, allowing him to roam forward knowing there was at least some cover behind him. Djalma was more of a 'they shall not pass' full back, but he also adapted to the new formation and became a little more adventurous. The new style allowed for the sublime balance of resilience and creativity that washed away the opposition at the 1958 World Cup Finals, and both Nílton and Djalma were still in place in Chile in 1962 to pick up a second winner's medal.

Flying full backs have remained a feature of Brazilian play throughout the years, but these two paved the way. Both, coincidentally, died in 2013, as did the custodian behind them, Gilmar. At least they were spared the sight of the 2014 full backs being so cruelly exposed by the Germans.

Solidity rating: maybe try the middle?

DUNCAN EDWARDS

(England, Defensive Midfielder)

To illustrate how much of a loss to football was Duncan Edwards, compare his career to a rough contemporary, Scotland's Dave Mackay. Mackay and Edwards were similar players with the best teams north and south of the border. They were half backs, as holding midfield players were then called. Both were exceptional in the tackle and effective at using the ball, and both were inspiring characters to their colleagues – resolute and unflinching. Both chipped in with the odd goal, and both were highly intelligent and modest.

When Edwards was killed in the 1958 Munich air crash, Mackay was busy leading Heart of Midlothian to the Scottish league title, their third (they won again in 1960 and that was that).

Edwards was only twenty-one when he died, along with seven of his playing colleagues and fifteen others. He was already a regular in the England side and a cornerstone of the 'Busby Babes'; had Edwards and his fellow casualties Roger Byrne and Tommy Taylor been spared, England might have fared better in the 1958 World Cup. It is not much of a leap to imagine Edwards as part of the 1966 England World Cup winning side.

Mackay moved to England to join Tottenham in 1959 and two years later was a key factor in Bill Nicholson's double-winning team. Mackay was still going a decade later as an influential veteran in Brian Clough's revival of

Derby County, whom Mackay later led to the league title as manager.

Edwards and Mackay were similar players but whose careers followed different paths: one utterly tragic, one an unqualified success. Ask any football fan or contemporary who was the better player, and you'll get the same answer. So if Mackay was a great player (and he was), just how good could Duncan Edwards have been? We'll never know.

Solidity rating: brains and brawn combined make a formidable obstacle.

TONY ADAMS

(England, Central Defender)

For a footballer who was once subjected to donkey noises every time he touched the ball (after he scored both goals in a 1-1 draw with Manchester United), Tony Adams made quite a career for himself. He played well over 600 matches for his only club, Arsenal, and retired at thirty-six after skippering the side to their second double in four years in 2002.

It wasn't always that rosy. After a promising start, Adams career faltered as he began drinking heavily; he later confessed to having trained and played while under the influence, and was involved in a number of booze-fuelled incidents, one of which resulted in a short jail sentence for drunk-driving.

That he sorted his life out and became more self-analytical is to his credit – his autobiography, *Addicted* (1998) was an interesting insight into both drink addiction and professional football. The resurrected Adams, under Arsène Wenger's astute management, improved as a player in the latter phase of his career. He won back his England place and enjoyed an outstanding World Cup alongside Sol Campbell in 1998. The donkey noises stopped.

At Arsenal, Adams led one of the great back lines in English domestic football history: David Seaman in goal, Lee Dixon and Nigel Winterburn at full back and Adams in the middle with Martin Keown. They didn't need that much pace, thanks to an understanding honed by training and discipline. One-nil to the Arsenal became a by-word under George Graham and the solidity continued under Wenger. After they all left between 2000 and 2004, the Arsenal back line has never quite been the same.

Solidity rating: improves as it matures but keep away from strong liquids.

PHILIPP LAHM

(Germany, Full Back/Defensive Midfielder)

The 2014 World Cup was the best World Cup of the last thirty years – great football played in the main in a good spirit with the best (and most entertaining) team winning the trophy. They had the best captain, too, a model of professionalism and reliability.

Philipp Lahm started the tournament playing in a holding midfield role, but moved back to his more familiar full-back position when defensive frailties emerged. This was the position he played in the extraordinary 7-1 demolition of Brazil and again in the final against Argentina, where he looked totally composed.

There is little flamboyant about Lahm but he's really good at defending and, given that is his job, that makes him a really good player. Tackling, marking, anticipating, playing the ball out of trouble, all those basic skills the Brazilians forgot in that semi-final, Lahm has in abundance. The same skills serve him well in that defensive midfield role, but there he is simply an excellent player, not a great one.

Lahm retired from international football after the World Cup but carried on as captain of Bayern Munich

(his only club) and continued to add to his already
bulky medal collection. He will never win the European
Championship winner's medal he needs for a full set but
he has a place at right back in the All-Time World XI.

Solidity rating: obdurate and reliable if used in the
correct way.

Sustainables

Football history is littered with talents who burned briefly, but were unable to sustain their brilliance, or showed great promise that they were never able to fulfil. This group represents the opposite: elements who were able to maintain efficiency and excellence long after their sell-by date indicated they should be discarded. Some were able to adapt to a different role in their later years, some substituted the vigour and energy of their youth with creativity and superior know-how in the latter stages of their career. Others, like Bobby Charlton, survived a scare which might have finished a lesser man and carried on to enjoy fantastic careers.

Column 6

21　　2/3 **S** Santos	25　　7 **Mw** Matthews	29　　4 **Bl** Blanchflower
22　　6 **Ed** Edwards	26　　9 **Ct** Charlton	30　　10 **Wa** Walter
23　　6 **Am** Adams	27　　1 **Sn** Shilton	31　　9 **Mi** Milla
24　　16 **Lh** Lahm	28　　11 **Gg** Giggs	32　　3 **Md** Maldini

25   7
Mw
Matthews

STANLEY MATTHEWS

(England, Winger)

Long before it was an accepted fact that people can continue competing into middle age, this player was trotting out to play in England's top division past his fiftieth birthday.

Stanley Matthews was a winger and in his early days he relied on speed, balance and footwork to stand out, all of which he possessed in abundance. Unusually for a pre-war winger he would run at defenders and leave them trailing with a deft body swerve or a drop of the shoulder rather than slow down and invite the tackle.

Matthews was twenty-four and an England regular when the war came. He missed six prime years: who knows how many games he would have played otherwise. As professional football restarted, his relationship with the Stoke board and management became fractious – the great man had a combative attitude to getting his dues – and he left to join Blackpool, where he had been stationed during the war. Matthews's FA Cup exploits became legend, losing two finals in 1948 and 1951 but finally winning the coveted medal (his only major trophy) in 1953 after a stunning comeback against Bolton. Although his England colleague Stan Mortensen scored a hat-trick, it was Matthews's running rings around the Bolton full back Tommy Banks that led to the game becoming known as the 'Matthews Final'.

Matthews had more freedom at Blackpool than at Stoke, often cutting in to use his clever passing ability rather than just taking on the full back every time he got the ball. Tom Finney at Preston had a similar style, playing more like a support striker than a conventional winger. Finney or Matthews became a regular debate of the time: they were both terrific players, with Matthews the greater all-round creativity and Finney the more potent goalscorer.

Matthews made an England comeback in 1953 and was England's best player at the 1954 World Cup Finals, where they lost to a strong Uruguay side. Matthews should probably have gone to the 1958 tournament, where England were poor, but he played his last international in 1957, aged forty-two. He remains both England's oldest footballer and the player with the longest international career, spanning twenty-two years.

Matthews dropped down a division in 1961 when he returned to Stoke, his hometown club. Were the years taking their toll? Not a bit – Matthews helped Tony Waddington's side gain promotion and he made more appearances in the top flight before finally bowing out at fifty-two.

Both illuminating and durable, this element will continue to give pleasure long after many others fade and disintegrate.

BOBBY CHARLTON

(England, Forward)

Bobby Charlton didn't just survive the Munich Air Disaster: he was one of the lucky ones, recovering completely and enjoying a long and fruitful career. Commentators have always liked to label players but Charlton wasn't a conventional winger, a midfielder or an attacker. He enjoyed a free role for club and country, running at defences from deep positions and unleashing fierce shots with either foot.

Charlton should have played in the 1958 World Cup: he travelled as a squad member but wasn't picked. England made changes halfway through the tournament but inexplicably chose Liverpool's Alan A'Court, a humdrum player, and uncapped Chelsea winger Peter Brabrook ahead of Charlton. No wonder Alf Ramsey insisted on control of selection when he took over as England manager. Charlton did play in 1962 when

England missed out; they lost to Hungary in their opening match and this meant they met Brazil in the quarter-final, when the other half of the draw would have presented a much clearer run.

No matter, for there was 1966 and home advantage, something England made full use of. After England squeezed past Argentina in an ugly quarter-final match it was Charlton who ensured their place in the final with two goals against Portugal – hardly anyone else played well that day, on either side.

His final England game – a then record 106th cap – was a less happy memory, as Charlton was substituted by Alf Ramsey in England's 3-2 defeat by West Germany in the 1970 World Cup. Ramsey was pilloried for the decision (Charlton was playing well), but it was an extremely hot day and the manager could make a case for bringing off his oldest player at 2-1 up.

Charlton's team, Manchester United, won the title in 1965 and 1967 – Charlton was just too young to have played in the winning fifties sides – and added the European Cup in 1968; the maestro stayed another five years but left when a fading team were relegated. His forays into management were not a success and he returned to United as a director in 1984, a post he holds until this day.

Charlton was always going to be a footballer – his uncle was Newcastle and England legend Jackie Milburn – and he turned out to be a model professional. He played the game fairly, in the right spirit and always downplayed his own contribution. A proper gentleman.

A tough and hardy element, will survive the most extreme tests.

PETER SHILTON

(England, Goalkeeper)

Shilton, or 'Shilts' as he is fondly known, was picked by Leicester as a teenage prodigy (unusual for a goalkeeper) and showed such promise the club sold Gordon Banks, the England No.1 and best goalkeeper in the world by now. He made his debut for England three years later, though it took him another decade to cement the spot as his own.

England had a glut of good keepers at the time. When Banks retired, England could call on Shilton, Liverpool's Ray Clemence, Joe Corrigan of Manchester City and Phil Parkes at QPR but it was Shilton and Clemence who vied for the jersey – at one point Ron Greenwood picked them in alternate matches. It took Shilton into the next decade to settle the argument with some fine displays at the 1982 World Cup. He would play in two more World Cups, reaching the quarter-final and semi-final in 1986 and 1990 respectively.

Shilton initially took the same club path as Banks, moving from Leicester to Stoke, but his next move to Nottingham Forest saw Shilton achieving club success that his predecessor never enjoyed. Under Brian Clough, Shilton was part of a team that won the league title and successive European Cups. Personal issues saw him move down to Southampton and later Derby County, but all the while he remained England's No.1, becoming a better keeper than ever in his late thirties. Never the best on crosses, he improved his decision making in this area, while never losing the bravery and agility that made him an outstanding shot-stopper.

In 1989 Shilton passed Bobby Moore's record of 108 caps for England (he finally reached 125) and he played at the 1990 World Cup aged forty, the competition's oldest captain to date. He passed 1,000 league matches playing for Orient in 1996, although this felt a little artificial: his competitive career had really ended at Derby, and had been followed by an uncomfortable foray into management at Plymouth before returning to playing.

Not the most attractive but redoubtable and hard-wearing.

RYAN GIGGS

(Wales, Winger/Midfielder)

Who has made the most Premier League appearances (632)? Who has appeared in the most consecutive Premier League seasons (22)? Who has scored in the most consecutive Premier League seasons (21)? Who has the most Premier League winner's medals (13)? The answer to all of the above is Ryan Giggs.

It's an impressive set of statistics. To have played right at the top for that long you have to look after yourself. Giggs's fitness and professionalism are a genuine marvel. Another surprising statistic is that he played only sixty-four games for Wales: it was always a bone of contention with Welsh managers and fans that Giggs never appeared to have the same commitment to his country. He rarely turned up for friendlies, although one suspects Alex Ferguson was protecting his charge from injury. Giggs suffered the curse of great players who played for countries that struggle to be competitive – Jari Litmanen (Finland) and George Weah (Liberia) would understand.

Giggs started his career as a winger whose pace and close control left top-class defenders floundering in his wake. His end product needed improvement and got it, but Giggs's ability to turn mundane possession into goal chances was exciting and invaluable. The goal that sticks in the mind was the winner in the FA Cup semi-final replay against Arsenal in 1999, United's treble year. United were down to ten men and tiring in extra time when Giggs seized on a poor pass and ran more than half the length of the field, before beating Arsenal's entire defence to score. And it was no ordinary defence Giggs cleaved through: this was the Arsenal of Dixon, Adams, Keown and Winterburn.

In later years, Giggs played more centrally and became a prompter and playmaker as his pace became less incendiary. His distribution improved and his ability to pick a pass was nearly the equal of his distinguished former teammate Paul Scholes. A great.

An adaptable element with many uses, if treated carefully.

Column 7

			33 Sb − Sebes
25 Mw 7 Matthews	29 Bl 4 Blanchflower	34 Rm 2 Ramsey	
26 Ct 9 Charlton	30 Wa 10 Walter	35 Sk − Shankly	
27 Sn 1 Shilton	31 Mi 9 Milla	36 Mv − Milutinović	
28 Gg 11 Giggs	32 Md 3 Maldini	37 Fg − Ferguson	

29	4
BI	
Blanchflower	

DANNY BLANCHFLOWER

(Northern Ireland, Playmaker)

It is well known that Danny Blanchflower was a terrific player and captain of Spurs's double-winning side of 1961: what is less remembered is that this season was the twilight of Blanchflower's career, a reward for his impressive longevity and consistency.

Belfast-born Blanchflower cut his teeth in England, in the second division with Barnsley, before Aston Villa picked him up. Things moved at a less hectic pace in the fifties and Blanchflower was twenty-five before he made his top-flight debut.

Bill Nicholson needed a leader for his Spurs team and saw in Blanchflower the kind of footballing brain that could make an entire team tick (indeed, he could equally well sit in the Conductors section of this table). Success was a while coming and it was only when Nicholson added Dave Mackay and John White to the midfield that everything clicked into place. Blanchflower's playmaking skills were maximised, and success finally arrived in spectacular fashion with the first double of the twentieth century. It was also the last occasion on which Tottenham won the league.

Blanchflower was captain of one of Northern Ireland's best sides, too. They weren't expected to qualify for the 1958 World Cup as Italy were in their group but a surprise defeat for the Italians in Portugal meant that, if the Ulstermen could beat Italy in Belfast, they would qualify.

The initial game was called off because the referee was fog-bound in Budapest. The teams played a friendly, instead, though the game was anything but as the crowd turned ugly. The situation was only defused when Blanchflower instructed his team to escort the visitors off the pitch.

The Irish won the rearranged game 2-1 and Northern Ireland went on to perform admirably in the quarter-finals, although they were beaten by France.

Blanchflower became an articulate and intelligent writer on football after his retirement.

Ideal for companion planting. Long lived.

FRITZ WALTER

(Germany, Playmaker)

One of the best young players to emerge in the pre-war years was Fritz Walter, an attacking inside forward with 1. FC Kaiserslautern. Walter made his debut in the national side in 1940 but two years later football was cancelled by the Nazis and most of the players were drafted into the military. Walter was captured on the Eastern Front during the war and only escaped deportation to a Soviet Gulag by the intervention of a Hungarian guard who recognised him by his football skills. (Only about 10 per cent of those taken ever came back from the Gulags.)

After the war, Walter resumed his club career and in 1951 earned a recall to the national side – the team having resumed playing internationals, now as West Germany, the year before. Walter was a terrific player, with great passing skills, good vision and an eye for goal, and at thirty-four years old, and now captain, he was to achieve his greatest moment.

At the 1954 World Cup, a West Germany sporting a number of changes from their usual starting eleven were trounced 8-3 by Hungary in a group match. West Germany routed Turkey 7-2 in a play-off to progress: they beat fellow runners-up Yugoslavia and Austria in the quarters and semis to set up a final against Hungary, except this time fielding their first eleven.

The story goes that Walter smiled when he looked out of his window on the morning of the match and saw the rain falling. He loved playing in the wet and it suited the German's direct style far more than it suited the intricate game of the Hungarians.

Certainly, West Germany needed all their fortitude: they were 2-0 down after just eight minutes. Max Morlock gave them some hope with a goal two minutes later and Helmut Rahn, the Rot-Weiss Essen winger, restored parity before twenty minutes were out. For a moment it looked like the rematch might yield another eleven goals. But now the West Germans, revolving around the cultured skills of Walter, Morlock and the solidity of Horst Eckel at half back, were at least a match for Kocsis, Hidegkuti and Puskás.

In the second half they came under sustained pressure, but Rahn scored the decisive goal with six minutes left, cueing a piece of commentary that is as much a part of German football folklore as Kenneth Wolstenholme's 'They think it's all over... it is now' is for England. The game was, as the excellent 2004 film of the same name attests, the Miracle of Bern.

Fritz Walter may not be as well-known as Franz Beckenbauer, Lothar Matthäus or Jürgen Klinsmann, but his memory is revered in Germany – at the Italy v. USA World Cup match in 2006 in Kaiserslautern there was a minute's silence on the fourth anniversary of Walter's death in 2002.

Walter was contemplating retirement before the 1954 World Cup. By 1958 he was retired and had to be coaxed back by Sepp Herberger: he made his last appearance in the semi-final defeat by Sweden, aged thirty-eight.

ROGER MILLA

(Cameroon, Forward)

Albert Roger Mooh Miller, real and full name, is a name more in keeping with the cartoon nature of the career of Roger Milla, as he is more commonly known.

Milla began his football in Cameroon, before earning a move to France in 1977. He spent seven years forging a career in France before a good spell at Saint-Étienne (during which they won back their place in the top division) raised his profile. After three years at Montpellier, in 1989 he dropped down a level to play for JS Saint-Pierroise in Réunion, the French territory in the Indian Ocean.

Now the fun started: Cameroon qualified for the 1990 World Cup Finals, but they were a bit light up front. Milla had appeared in Cameroon's first World Cup campaign in 1982 (they failed to get past the group stage, drawing all three games), but retired from internationals in 1987. The Cameroon President (of the country, not the football federation) called the thirty-eight-year-old to ask if he could return to play for his country one more time.

Cameroon beat Argentina in their first match, despite finishing with nine men (Benjamin Massing's tackle on Caniggia was worthy of assault charges). With half an hour to go in their second game against a strong Romanian side featuring Hagi, Popescu and Dumitrescu, the score was goalless. Enter Milla, and one goal from a bad piece of defending and another rampant finish from a good knock-down left Cameroon 2-0 up. They qualified for the next round as group winners.

Against Colombia, Milla scored twice in extra time sending Cameroon through as the first African side to reach the last eight. By now Milla's little victory wiggle by the corner flag had become a cause célèbre and the veteran was an international celebrity.

Against England, Milla nearly did it again, coming off the bench to win a penalty and set up what looked like a win – until two Gary Lineker spot-kicks turned the tie around.

Four years later, the oldest man to score in a World Cup Finals game broke his own record when he scored against Russia aged forty-two. Unfortunately, this Cameroon team were a shadow of the 1990 team: Oleg Salenko scored five goals for Russia and Cameroon went home early. But Milla never stopped smiling, and we got to see the wiggle once again.

Milla is one of the great footballing characters – not a great player, just a really good one. He deservedly won the African Player of the Century award, an accolade awarded as much for his charm, durability and the joy he brought to playing as for pure ability.

This element can remain dormant for years before revealing its spectacular effervescence.

PAOLO MALDINI

(Italy, Left Back/Central Defender)

Paolo Maldini is one of the best defenders to have ever played the game. Former Milan legend Nils Liedholm (of 'Gre-No-Li' fame) gave him his debut as a sixteen-year-old, but Maldini had football in his genetic make-up; his father, Cesare, was a fine defender for Milan and Italy in the sixties.

Maldini played for nine managers at Milan and five for the national side (including his father in both roles). He started his career as a full back, quickly moving to the now familiar left side as he was a genuinely two-footed player. He made his debut for Italy in 1988 and was part of a Milan back four (Tassotti–Costacurta–Baresi–Maldini) that could lay claim to being the best club defence in history.

By the turn of the century, Maldini was increasingly deployed as a centre half. Franco Baresi had retired and Maldini had lost some of his former pace. He had such a good football brain that he noticeably changed his style when he changed position, committing less to the tackle and relying more on positioning and timing. In his pomp, Maldini was the complete defender; quick, strong, intelligent and utterly professional.

The biggest prizes in international football eluded Maldini. He played in the 1994 World Cup final but a dull game against Brazil was settled on penalties and two other great Italian players, Roberto Baggio and Franco Baresi, missed their kicks to hand the trophy to the South Americans. Club success was a very different matter. Maldini played in a staggering eight European Cup and Champions League finals from 1989 to 2007, the last when his side gained revenge over Liverpool for their defeat on penalties two years earlier. Only players from the legendary Real Madrid side in the early days of the competition can match this. The same period brought him seven *Serie A* titles and a record number of appearances in the top division – a record unlikely to be beaten anytime soon unless Francesco Totti keeps going into his forties!

This element is hard-wearing and will work in all conditions.

Conductors

Conductors are conduits for the better performance of others; they take the charge generated by talented players and turn it into something more formidable.

Sometimes a club or country can accrue all the right elements or components, but the man in charge does not have the know-how or instinct to allow the talents to flow in the right direction and produce success. This is why the position of manager, or coach as they tend to be called outside the UK, is so crucial. While the players are responsible for their own level of performance, the manager can help them produce their best by setting the team up tactically. Many managers and coaches were no more than ordinary performers, but they learned the knack of lining up elements in such a way that their effectiveness is maximised. It is back to that crucial question of balance again.

Column 8

33 Sb — Sebes		**38** Me — Meisl
29 Bl 4 Blanchflower	**34** Rm 2 Ramsey	**39** Bb — Busby
30 Wa 10 Walter	**35** Sk — Shankly	**40** Js — Stein
31 Mi 9 Milla	**36** Mv — Milutinović	**41** Cl 9 Clough
32 Md 3 Maldini	**37** Fg — Ferguson	**42** Gu 4 Guardiola

33   –

Sb

Sebes

GUSTÁV SEBES

(Hungary, Coach)

In the years immediately after the war, Gusztáv Sebes rose to prominence in the Hungarian Communist Party. By 1949 he had acquired the position of Deputy Minister for Sport, which in effect meant he was manager and coach of the national team. Sebes himself was not especially gifted as a coach, but he was adept at spotting and adopting clever innovations and tactics used by others.

At MTK Budapest, manager Márton Bukovi regularly deployed Péter Palotás or Nándor Hidegkuti as a deep-lying centre forward. Rather than playing as the spearhead of the attack as was the accepted manner, the number nine would drop behind the two inside forwards, confusing the opposing centre half and often drawing him out of position. At the same time, one of the two half backs, the old-style midfield players, would hover just in front of the defence, becoming almost a fourth member of that unit.

Many Hungarian teams, including the national team under Sebes, adopted this formation that was nearer to 4-2-4 than the more traditional formation of 3-2-5 (or 'WM' as many commentators now prefer).

Hungary achieved unprecedented success with these methods. They became the first continental side to beat England at Wembley in 1953 and followed that up by inflicting what remains England's worst ever defeat, a 7-1 thrashing in Budapest the following spring. At the 1954 World Cup they came incredibly close to lifting the trophy, beating favourites Brazil and champions Uruguay before falling at the final hurdle to a well drilled and underrated West Germany team.

The crushing of the 1956 uprising by the Soviets led to many defections among senior players and defeats against Turkey and Belgium in the same year led to Sebes's dismissal.

Sebes was gone but his tactics lived on. When one of his acolytes, Béla Guttman, deployed it in Brazil during a coaching stint the following year, the seeds were sown for the creation of one of the most brilliant teams ever seen. Not only did Sebes oversee one of the most inventive and talented European teams ever seen, he indirectly helped create an even greater South American one.

Sebes's Theory of Creativity: the Party does not approve of individualism and creativity – unless they win football matches against the feckless and decadent West.

ALF RAMSEY

(England, Defender, Manager)

Alf Ramsey: tactical genius or curmudgeonly try-hard who happened to get a talented group of players together for one World Cup, and benefited from some generous refereeing and home support?

The answer is a bit of both. Ramsey played against Hungary in 1953 (see Sebes above) and was also an integral part of Bill Nicholson's Tottenham side of the 1950s. While he was indeed a curmudgeon and deeply suspicious of foreigners (witness his offensive over-reaction after the rough-house game with Argentina in 1966) he was also smart enough to absorb some of the lessons learned.

He was a good enough manager to win the league title with an ordinary Ipswich team in 1962 and seemed a solid choice for England: 'establishment enough', but also man enough to dictate his terms, which included team selection (the previous manager, Walter Winterbottom, had suffered from the baffling choices made by an arbitrary selection committee).

Ramsey did the simple things well, just as he had as a tough full back. He picked the best players, gave them a system and told them to keep hold of the ball. He added a couple of quirky choices and ignored popular but outdated opinion that you still had to play wingers to win football matches. It worked.

England won the World Cup in 1966 with just three world-class players (Banks, Moore, Bobby Charlton), and a couple of good youngsters (Ball and Peters). An even better squad might have reached the final four years later, but instead let their manager down with a careless half hour against West Germany.

When the other sides surpassed England and they failed to qualify for the 1974 World Cup, Ramsay got the sack. But he left a legacy of expectation that has remained unfulfilled for fifty years.

Alf's Theory of Width: width is obsolete in the presence of two Bobbys.

35	–
Sk	
Shankly	

BILL SHANKLY

(Scotland, Manager)

Is it entirely coincidental that the four most revered club managers in Britain since the Second World War have all been Scottish? Probably. With apologies to Messrs Nicholson, Ramsey, Clough, Paisley, Robson and Wenger, the four men in question are Matt Busby and Alex Ferguson at Manchester United, Bill Shankly at Liverpool and Jock Stein at Celtic.

Bill Shankly was in charge of second division Huddersfield Town when Liverpool expressed an interest in employing him. Frustrated by the Yorkshire club's lack of ambition Shankly accepted the offer three days after Liverpool lost to Huddersfield in a league match. This was 1959: Liverpool earned promotion three years later and won the league title in 1964. Huddersfield won nothing.

Shankly's programme was a long-term plan, and involved faith in a youth system that by the 1960s had started to produce a crop of good players to go with those he bought. He was fortunate in having a club that had experienced some tough times and was prepared to give him space and time to fulfil his vision. Shankly set up a great scouting system, run by Geoff Twentyman, and was rewarded with players like Emlyn Hughes, Kevin Keegan and Ray Clemence; this scouting network performed the same service for his successors.

Shankly's legacy wasn't just success. It was also continuity, setting up a system that could be passed on with minimum disruption. Bob Paisley won many more trophies than Shankly, but he could not have achieved it without the infrastructure he inherited. Much is made of 'The Boot Room', a scruffy old room the management team used to meet in and discuss football matters. Graeme Souness was pilloried for scrapping the meetings and changing the room, but that is missing the point. Souness just wasn't as good a manager. It wasn't the room, it was the people, and foremost among them was Bill Shankly. What wouldn't Liverpool and Steven Gerrard have given for some of that continuity over the last twenty years?

Shankly's Theory of Management: wisdom kept all to oneself is simply self-regard.

BORA MILUTINOVIĆ

(Yugoslavia, Coach)

A blow-by-blow account of Velibor 'Bora' Milutinović's managerial career could fill all the pages in this book – he has had sixteen jobs in a thirty-year career and is one of two managers to have taken five teams to World Cup Finals tournaments (the other being Carlos Alberto Parreira).

Milutinović's charges were: Mexico, the hosts in 1986. They reached the quarter-final where even some blatant refereeing couldn't prevent them losing on penalties; Costa Rica (for the first time) in 1990, who got out of a tricky group by beating Sweden and Scotland before losing to a strong Czechoslovakia side; United States, the hosts in 1994, who eliminated highly fancied Colombia, got to the second phase and were knocked out by eventual champions Brazil; Nigeria, who looked to be a talented side in 1998 with Jay-Jay Okocha *et al*. They beat Spain to reach the second round, but failed to show up against Denmark and got hammered by the Laudrup-led side; and China in 2002, which is the only time a Milutinović team has gone out in the group phase.

This is a fine record. Most of these sides lacked superstars and were completely unfancied. The United States fed off this achievement and have become a perennial thorn in the side of the established teams in the finals ever since. Only Nigeria disappointed, but they have proved flaky a number of times, not just in 1998.

Bora's Theory of Achievement: even the tiniest cup can runneth over.

37   –
Fg
Ferguson

ALEX FERGUSON

(Scotland, Manager)

Ferguson is the most successful coach in the history of British football. He may have been a bit grumpy and churlish on occasion, and was 'nae too good' at accepting criticism, but you can't argue with his record.

Ferguson took a club that was living on its manky laurels and turned them into serial winners both at home and abroad. And he did it again and again and again.

Even before the United job, Alex Ferguson was an achiever: his Aberdeen side won the Scottish League in 1979–80 – the club's second title and their first for twenty-five years. They added two more while he was there and haven't won again since he left. He also brought Aberdeen their first and only European trophy, beating mighty Real Madrid in the 1983 Cup Winners' Cup final. No that wasn't a typo: Aberdeen beat Real Madrid.

Ferguson's record at United is well documented: thirteen league titles starting in 1993 and ending in 2013, the year he retired.

There were some brilliant transfer coups along the way, not all of them expensive: Peter Schmeichel and Denis Irwin cost less than a million; Eric Cantona, Ole Gunnar Solskjaer and Edwin van der Sar were under two million and even the £12.5 million paid for teenager Cristiano Ronaldo was made to look like a bargain (he was subsequently sold to Real Madrid for £80 million). There were less successful ones too – Massimo Taibi, Eric Djemba-Djemba and Juan Sebastián Verón and a sweary response to criticism of the latter showed Ferguson's truculent side. Maybe he was so used to extracting the best from his charges that he found failures difficult to stomach.

Ferguson was a brilliant motivator and he put out teams that played fantastic attacking football. The talent that came out of United in the 1990s – Giggs, Scholes, Beckham, the Neville brothers, Nicky Butt – was a throwback to the halcyon days of the Busby Babes. Maybe it was fate's way of showing what Busby's side might have achieved had the Munich crash not happened. No wonder even an accomplished manager like David Moyes found the shoes a bit big.

Alex's Theory of Everlasting Success: let us not accept defeat with grace, for by that token are we weak and downtrodden. Let us instead do the trampling.

Column 9

33 Sb Sebes –	**38** Me Meisl –	
34 Rm Ramsey 2	**39** Bb Busby –	**43** Mz Meazza 8
35 Sk Shankly –	**40** Js Stein –	**44** Li Liedholm 10
36 Mv Milutinović –	**41** Cl Clough 9	**45** Sm Schmeichel 1
37 Fg Ferguson –	**42** Gu Guardiola 4	**46** Xi Xavi 6

HUGO MEISL

(Austria, Coach)

Hugo Meisl was the architect of *Das Wunderteam*, an excellent Austria side of the 1920s and 1930s. He was also a force in central European football more generally: he initiated the Mitropa Cup, an international competition based in that region and oversaw the introduction of professional football in Austria.

Meisl was friendly with the influential Scottish coach Jimmy Hogan, and admired Hogan's commitment to a game based on short passing interchanges rather than individual dribbling or crossing for the centre forward to try and head a goal. He built an Austrian team around this method, with the brilliant Matthias Sindelar at the heart. They played a traditional formation with half backs, an old-fashioned centre half and wingers, but their ability to control and retain the ball presaged some of the great teams to come, especially the Hungarians of the 1950s.

Austria went unbeaten for fourteen games from 1931, including two defeats of neighbouring Germany and a 5-0 rout of Scotland, a formidable side in that era. The run was ended with a 4-3 defeat by England at Wembley, but the Austrians showed they could match England at a venue where the hosts would remain unbeaten for another twenty years. Meisl's gifted and technical side went on to reach the World Cup semi-finals in 1934 and the Olympic final two years later, losing to Italy on both occasions.

Hugo Meisl died of a heart attack in 1937; he was an Austrian Jew and was spared the depredations of the *Anschluss* (the German annexation of Austria) and the concentration camps.

Hugo's Law of Anti-Aerodynamics: if the ball is kicked into the air, the percentage chance of it not coming back increases threefold.

39	–
Bb	
Busby	

MATT BUSBY

(Scotland, Manager)

Matt Busby's twenty-five years at Manchester United can only be counted as an unqualified success. He won United's first league title in forty-one years in 1951–2 (after four near misses as runners-up in the post-war years). Over the next five years Busby developed a dominant side (back-to-back league championships in 1956 and 1957) without spending any money, such was the production line of talent the Old Trafford club was producing: Duncan Edwards, David Pegg, Roger Byrne, and Bobby Charlton among them. He paid significant fees for only two of his best players: goalkeeper Harry Gregg and centre forward Tommy Taylor.

Then in February 1958 came the Munich air disaster. Busby suffered terrible injuries and felt responsible for the deaths of his charges. He thought seriously about resigning but he was back at the helm at the start of the following season, thinking about how to rebuild his 'Babes' around the survivors – Gregg, Charlton, Dennis Viollet, Bill Foulkes – and how to integrate the hastily assembled patchwork of players assistant Jimmy Murphy had brought in. He replaced them gradually, bringing new players like Nobby Stiles and John Aston through the youth system and adding carefully chosen transfer targets (Denis Law in 1962 and Paddy Crerand in 1963). A key addition was the young winger George Best, spotted as 'something special' by a United scout in Belfast.

The team got better and better and the league title was regained in 1965 and won again in 1967. The Holy Grail followed in 1968: the European Cup that United felt was their due, with Best inspiring United to a 4-1 win over Benfica in extra time to become the first English side to win the trophy. Imagine the emotion of Busby, Foulkes and Charlton.

Busby retired the following year after over two decades in charge but he stayed on in one capacity or another until his death in 1994. What a journey.

Busby's Theory of Childcare: why spend money when you can grow your own?

JOCK STEIN

(Scotland, Manager)

Strange as it seems given the dominance of Celtic and Rangers (and currently just Celtic) in Scottish domestic football, but in the years after the Second World War the destiny of the Scottish title was not a foregone conclusion. In the twenty years after the war there were seven winners of the Scottish League. In that time Celtic won it only once, in 1953–4, under the captaincy of the veteran Jock Stein.

Stein was forced through injury to retire soon after and went into management, first with Dunfermline and then Hibernian. It was inevitable he would end up back at Parkhead. There followed, from his appointment in 1965, ten league titles (including nine in succession), eight Scottish Cups and six Scottish League Cups.

The season of seasons was 1966–7. Amid winning the Scottish treble, Stein's team embarked on a European Cup campaign that started in Switzerland and ended in glory at the final in Lisbon. They won through four rounds of two-legged matches, losing only once, to Vojvodina in the quarter-final first leg. It took a last-minute goal from captain Billy McNeill in the second leg to down the Yugoslav champions. The final was played in Lisbon against Internazionale, a seasoned side full of Italian internationals. Celtic's task was made harder when they conceded a penalty inside the first ten minutes.

Now they had to play eighty minutes against Herrera's side, the masters of defend and counter-attack. Just after the hour, Tommy Gemmell equalised with a rocket-propelled drive – has there been another full back with such a good shot? – and if Steve Chalmers's late winner owed much to a sharp deflection, it was no more than Celtic deserved for an attacking display full of verve and passion.

Stein had won his immortality: the first manager to win the European Cup with a British club. Impressively, all eleven of the team were local, born within twenty miles of the ground. Stein's team continued to rack up trophies until a brief decline persuaded the Celtic directors to move him aside in favour of McNeill. A spell at Leeds didn't work out and Stein jumped at the chance to manage the Scotland team – in disarray after the 1978 World Cup debacle under Ally MacLeod.

Shortly after the final whistle in a vital qualification match against Wales for the 1986 World Cup, Stein suffered a massive heart attack. His assistant took the team to Mexico the following year – a young Aberdeen coach by the name of Alex Ferguson.

Stein was a hard, even harsh man. He expected utter loyalty from his players but didn't always reciprocate, and he had little time for other people's problems. Yet he achieved unprecedented success with a Scottish club, and his influence on the even more successful Ferguson, both in management and playing style, is manifest.

Jock's Law: 'The secret of being a good manager is to keep the six players who hate you away from the five who are undecided'. (This is an actual quote.)

41		9
	Cl	
	Clough	

BRIAN CLOUGH

(England, Forward, Manager)

The greatest manager England never had. Brian Clough thought so: 'I wouldn't say I was the best manager in the business, but I was in the top one.'

Many others would agree. Clough's brief and ignominious period as manager of the all-conquering

Leeds side gave a clue that he was not as comfortable or accomplished at dealing with prima donnas and egos as he was at moulding less talented but also less fractious individuals into a sleek unit.

Clough did great work, truly brilliant, at Derby County and Nottingham Forest, turning two unfashionable clubs into league winners and – in Forest's case – champions of Europe. He took players that other managers had made little of, like John Robertson and Kenny Burns, and turned them into world beaters. He instilled a desire and a work ethic in his teams that made them massively more than the sum of their parts. John McGovern and Ian Bowyer were good players, nothing more, but under Clough's tutelage they were an impregnable barrier in the midfield. Bruce Rioch was just Derby's token hard man until Clough's coaching made him a more rounded player.

All the time there was a restlessness in Clough – a need to do things his own style, the need to prove his doubters wrong. And that would never have sat with the 'suits' at the FA. The maverick selections would have been wilful and not always sensible. Key players would be alienated. The egos would have rebelled, just as they did at Leeds.

It wasn't to be, and rightly so. Better to be remembered as the best man never to get the job than the man who got the job and blew it – his predecessor at Leeds, Don Revie, might attest to that.

Cloughie's Law: never underestimate yourself.

PEP GUARDIOLA

(Spain, Defensive Midfielder/Coach)

Take Herbert Chapman's acumen and belief that everything stems from a sound back line and add Rinus Michels's understanding of space and fluidity and retention of the ball. What have you got? You pretty much have Pep Guardiola's Barcelona. Include a bit of pace and you have his Bayern Munich team.

Forget 'tiki-taka', Barcelona actually play a version of Total Football and have been doing so ever since the early 1990s under – surprise, surprise – Johan Cruyff. The accent on keeping the ball and keeping moving is not new, but Guardiola's team took it to singular heights.

Most other methods rely on strength and pace to a degree, but rule changes and greater protection for ball players meant Guardiola could assemble a team of gifted players that would have been untenable even ten years earlier. With the new offside rule (2005) Guardiola (and others) reasoned that the space on the pitch was now in front of the opponent's back line rather than behind it, and set his team up accordingly.

As a player, Guardiola was a terrific holding midfielder with Cruyff's team, playing for Barcelona between 1990 and 2001. (He also won forty-seven caps for Spain before pursuing a coaching career.)

He was only thirty-seven when he was given the Barcelona coaching job, one he did with remarkable success for four years before leaving for Bayern Munich and a new challenge. That Barcelona challenged Real Madrid's *galácticos* with a team made up largely of home-grown talent is in the main down to Guardiola.

He proclaims himself not a disciple of 'tiki-taka', a claim he backed up by winning trophies with Munich in a very different style – a style that is much more direct and suited to the players at his disposal. He is still only forty-four and already has done enough to be thought a great coach. In twenty years, he could be one of the very best, or maybe *the* very best.

Pep's Law: if you do not have all the elements for your preferred formula, change the formula to suit the elements you do have, not vice versa.

Catalysts

The Catalysts are the footballing elements whose individual style and performance enhance the style and performance of those around them. Some catalysts are unremarkable players on the surface of it, but who seem to bring out the best in their colleagues. Whether it is by leadership or by example or by a particularly inclusive method of playing the game, these elements all galvanise those around them into performing to their utmost. Compared to the Conductors their influence is felt more on the field and more directly.

Column 10

38 ⁻ **Me** Meisl		
39 ⁻ **Bb** Busby	**43** 8 **Mz** Meazza	**47** 10 **Sf** Schiaffino
40 ⁻ **Js** Stein	**44** 10 **Li** Liedholm	**48** 8 **Mh** Mühren
41 9 **Cl** Clough	**45** 1 **Sm** Schmeichel	**49** 10 **La** Laudrup
42 4 **Gu** Guardiola	**46** 6 **Xi** Xavi	**50** 10 **Bk** Bergkamp

GIUSEPPE MEAZZA

(Italy, Forward)

Giuseppe Meazza was Italy's most famous player in the years before the Second World War. He was the playmaker and talisman of the team: without him they would have been an orchestra without a lead violin.

He won two World Cups with the Azzurri and a handful of domestic trophies with Internazionale. Originally rejected by AC Milan for being too lightweight, AC Milan now play in a stadium (shared with local rivals Internazionale) named after the man they ignored (although he did have one brief season at Milan when he left Inter). The official name of the ground known as the San Siro is the Stadio Giuseppe Meazza.

Meazza had incredible balance and footwork. Stories abound of his tricks – Meazza's Wikipedia entry amusingly relates how he used to draw the goalkeeper out of his goal as a matador would a bull, before scoring with ease. Once he is alleged to have stopped the ball dead with his heel while running full pelt and watched two onrushing defenders collide with each other. It is possible the reporter got confused with an Abbott and Costello film.

Meazza was used by Mussolini's propaganda machine as a typical Italian alpha male. A notorious womaniser, he was often seen at disreputable nightclubs on the night before a game, dressed in a sharp suit and dancing the tango with a gardenia tucked behind his ear.

A Meazza (n); a hugely influential Italian footballer.

NILS LIEDHOLM

(Sweden, Attacking Midfielder)

This entry is headed as Nils Liedholm, but in truth could equally be about his compatriots Gunnar Gren and Gunnar Nordahl, with whom Liedholm formed the 'Gre-No-Li' trio that dominated Italian football in the early 1950s.

In 1949 AC Milan raided two Swedish clubs (Norrköping and Gothenburg) to sign these three attacking players. They were the catalyst that yielded Milan's first league title for forty-four years and older Milan fans remember the 'Gre-No-Li' with great affection. Absurdly the move saw them banned from playing for their country as Sweden had a strict amateur-only policy.

Gren and Liedholm were inside forwards. Gren played deeper and consequently scored fewer goals, but he was the prompter and the playmaker while the athletic Liedholm played what is now referred to as a box-to-box game. Liedholm was a fitness fanatic – he pursued various athletic disciplines to keep in shape – and he was adept at arriving late in the penalty area to get on the end of crosses (a sort of 1950s Frank Lampard or Michael Ballack). Nordahl was the goalscorer, a genuine number nine, tall and strong and powerful in the air. Even the prolific Andriy Shevchenko couldn't match his record 221 goals for Milan in all competitions.

With the 1958 World Cup approaching the Swedish authorities panicked. Their best players were all in Italy; Nordahl had retired in 1958 but Gren and Liedholm, together with the wingers Kurt Hamrin and Lennart Skoglund, and the centre half Bengt Gustavsson were all playing professionally. The authorities reluctantly caved in and the Swedes came home and added weight to a campaign that saw their team reach the final; no disgrace in being trounced by the 1958 Brazilian team. The mercurial Hamrin was the star of the show, but Gren (now thirty-seven) and Liedholm (thirty-five) played their full part.

Gre-No-Li: Sweden's most famous export after the Volvo.

PETER SCHMEICHEL

(Denmark, Goalkeeper)

Goalkeepers have different strengths and weaknesses. Peter Schmeichel was not as elastic or acrobatic as some other top-class keepers (he was a massive bloke, if not in the same class of bulk as William 'Fatty' Foulke), and early on in his career he was prone to unforced errors. But he was smart and learned to use his bulk to his advantage.

Schmeichel became the best, undisputedly, at racing off his line to block strikers free on goal. Even strikers of the quality of Shearer and Henry could be distracted by the sight of a six-foot-three brick of Danish goalkeeper rushing at them. Still balanced and still on his feet, Schmeichel would spread his enormous wingspan and show the attacker those huge hands. No wonder so many quailed and failed.

Schmeichel's anticipation was excellent and compensated for any lack of agility. He was as fearsome to his own defenders as he was to opposing strikers if he felt they were neglectful of their duty. The image of his face florid, roaring at Denis Irwin or Steve Bruce for some minor misdemeanour, was one of the sights of the first few years of the Premier League.

If the highlight of his international career came relatively early, when Denmark unexpectedly won the 1992 European Championship, his career-high at club level was in 1999 when Manchester United won the treble and Schmeichel, in his last season at the club, was named captain for the Champions League Final in Roy Keane's absence. It was his giant presence in the Bayern Munich penalty area (he once scored with a header in the dying minutes of a different Champions League match) that helped cause the mayhem and allowed Teddy Sheringham to score the equaliser. Alex Ferguson, who bought some tasty players in his time, rates

Schmeichel as the best buy he made: £500,000 for a serial winner was good business.

The legacy lives on; Schmeichel's son, Kasper, has just completed an excellent first Premier league season with Leicester City. Kasper likes to do the big hands thing, just like his dad.

XAVI

(Spain, Midfield)

The Spanish side that won three major trophies from 2008 to 2012 have been overrated by the media. They were tough and excellent at retaining possession, but they lacked the incisive brilliance of the best Brazilian sides or of Barcelona, the premier club team. The tiki-taka version of total football they employed was used largely as a defensive mechanism to deny opponents possession and space; most football fans found it less enchanting than the media.

Reservations expressed. If you *were* going to play that style of football, you wanted Xavi in your team, especially if he had his teammate Andrés Iniesta alongside him. Xavi was the puppeteer, sitting deep and acting as the fulcrum, ready to take the ball when an attack broke down and begin the whirligig again. The understanding between Xavi and Iniesta was ingrained and instinctive; watching Barcelona or Spain it was amazing how often it seemed that they had played themselves into a hole only for one of these two to pop up and recycle the ball. They made themselves the ultimate slaves to the system.

It makes for an impressive CV when you win everything you enter, so maybe the reservations are unfair. But there must remain a suspicion that outside that unique Spanish moment Xavi and Iniesta would never have achieved so much.

Tiki + taka = 1,428 passes and no goals.

Column 11

43 **8** **Mz** Meazza	**47** **10** **Sf** Schiaffino	**51** – **Ch** Chapman
44 **10** **Li** Liedholm	**48** **8** **Mh** Mühren	**52** – **Mc** Michels
45 **1** **Sm** Schmeichel	**49** **10** **La** Laudrup	**53** – **Lb** Lobanovskyi
46 **6** **Xi** Xavi	**50** **10** **Bk** Bergkamp	**54** – **Wg** Wenger

47	10
Sf	
Schiaffino	

JUAN SCHIAFFINO

(Uruguay, Playmaker)

Uruguay were top drawer in the 1950s. They beat Brazil on their own turf to win the World Cup in 1950 and were easily the best South American side in Switzerland four years later, losing a slam-dunk classic 4-2 to Hungary.

Their best player was a tall, stately inside forward called Juan Alberto Schiaffino. This was a Uruguayan side content in the main to play football rather than resort to the intimidation tactics sometimes employed. All of which suited Schiaffino – his passing and vision were suited to a creative not a destructive game. Uruguay had exceptionally quick wingers, especially Alcides Ghiggia on the right, and it was Schiaffino's ability to release them with accurate fizzed passes that turned the tide in the 1950 final. Four years later the Peñarol playmaker was just as impressive as Uruguay beat Scotland 7-0 and brushed England aside on their way to the semi-finals and their showdown with Hungary.

That was the last of Schiaffino in the pale blue stripes; he signed for AC Milan, and as was the custom of the time, became an honorary Italian. He played only four more internationals but make no mistake: this was a truly great player, perhaps the least well known of the very top rank of players. Only two Uruguayan players have come close to this level since: the luckless Enzo Francescoli, who was surrounded in the main by second-raters and thugs, and Luis Suáraz.

Juan's Theory of Resolve: with garra (see Andrade), nothing is foretold and nothing is ever lost.

ARNOLD MÜHREN

(Holland, Midfielder)

When did foreign players become a popular investment in British football? In the late 1970s, when Ipswich Town bought first Arnold Mühren and then Frans Thijssen.

Ipswich Town were a force to be reckoned with in the late 1970s and early 1980s. They had a very astute manager in the former England international Bobby Robson and an excellent youth system that gave them a production line of quality young players. Ipswich won the FA Cup in 1978 and only once (that year, oddly) finished outside the top six between 1973 and 1982.

After the FA Cup victory Robson decided the team needed a little more sophistication. Robson was a long-time admirer of Dutch football, so he added Mühren, a cultured left midfielder with FC Twente. A year later he added another Twente player, Frans Thijssen, a more urgent and aggressive player than the graceful Mühren. They brought successive second-place finishes in the league, and the club won its only European trophy, the 1981 UEFA Cup, with the Dutchmen in the side. More importantly, along with Ossie Ardiles at Tottenham, they showed that the old adage that overseas players didn't have the stomach for the English league was false. Ardiles and compatriot Ricky Villa were the summer's most high-profile signings but Thijssen and Mühren had a greater effect on their team's style.

A thirty-seven year-old Mühren moved to Manchester United and won his place back in the Holland team, just in time to win a European Championship medal in 1988, while Thijssen spent time in the US before returning to Holland.

Robson became the England manager but he returned to club football to enjoy major success at Eindhoven and Barcelona before finishing his career with Newcastle.

Bobby Robson's love affair with Dutch football continued when he was appointed manager of PSV Eindhoven after leaving the England job. They won the *Eredivisie* (Dutch top flight) both seasons he was in charge.

49   10

La

Laudrup

MICHAEL LAUDRUP

(Denmark, Attacking Midfielder)

Denmark were no great shakes as a footballing nation until the last twenty years. There was a great sweeper, Morten Olsen, who is rightly remembered as a father figure to the modern generation, but it was Michael Laudrup who made Danish football sexy and became the yardstick for the next generation to try and match.

Michael Laudrup, the elder of two footballing brothers, was a craftsman, a playmaker, with vision and great passing ability, which he used to great effect in Johan Cruyff's Barcelona 'Dream Team' of the early 1990s. Brother Brian was a winger, a quick, elusive forward with a keen eye for goal. He was a cut above those around him in his successful spell under Graeme Souness at Rangers.

After they retired the brothers followed different paths, just as they did while they were playing: Michael went into management (and brought Swansea their first major trophy) while Brian spends his time as a summariser for Danish TV.

Michael was the superior player overall, but fell out with the Danish coach and didn't take part in their victorious European Championship campaign of 1992. Brian did and it is the one area where his CV betters his sibling's.

In domestic football Michael won league titles in Italy (with Juventus), Spain (with both Barça and Real, including four consecutive wins with the Dream Team) and also Holland (with Ajax). Add in the 1992 European Cup and this easily tops Brian's single *Serie A* (AC Milan) and three Scottish titles.

Michael returned to the national side after his hissy fit and the brothers made a joint farewell at the 1998 World Cup Finals. It was a good send-off, as Denmark soundly beat a much-touted Nigerian side before falling 3-2 to Brazil in a classic match.

Thankfully, these two are not the same Brian & Michael who assaulted our ears with 'Matchstalk Men and Matchstalk Cats and Dogs', which reached No. 1 in the UK in 1978.

DENNIS BERGKAMP

(Holland, Forward)

For a player who lacked a yard of pace (certainly for a striker), wasn't that good in the air and looked as if a stiff wind might knock him over, Dennis Bergkamp enjoyed a decent career! The man who became known as the Non-Flying Dutchman remains one of the very best to grace the Premier League and the international stage.

Bergkamp may not have been the quickest, but he was one of the smartest. Ostensibly a centre forward, he played deeper and deeper throughout his career, wandering into areas defenders daren't follow and using his exquisite touch and intuitive passing to make space and then release others.

His understanding at Arsenal with his compatriot Marc Overmars and Frenchman Thierry Henry was of enormous benefit to both. One of the reasons Henry was never quite as effective for France was their lack of a player like Bergkamp: Zidane was a much more direct and selfish player.

Bergkamp's finest moment was his last-minute winning goal against Argentina in a World Cup quarter-final in 1998. Frank de Boer hit a brilliant, raking sixty-yard pass which Bergkamp cushioned and killed on his instep with enviable ease. He cut inside Roberto Ayala (no slouch) and dinked the ball past Carlos Roa with the outside of his foot. It was unbelievable skill and Bergkamp made it look effortless. A great and often underrated player.

Bergkamp's fear of flying is well-known. When he signed for Arsenal he settled for a slightly smaller salary in exchange for a clause that permitted him to miss European games that necessitated a flight.

Transmuters

Some elements aren't just a catalyst for change within their team or club, but within the game. Their contribution is so far-reaching and memorable that it changed the nature of the game for good, whether on a local or international level, or both.

Whether by innovative tactics, new methods by which they run a team or a club, or changes to the laws and the way the game is marketed and presented, these elements – the Transmuters – had a lasting effect on the game, leaving a legacy well beyond the end of their career or involvement.

Column 12

47 10 **Sf** Schiaffino	51 – **Ch** Chapman	55 – **Rt** Rimet
48 8 **Mh** Mühren	52 – **Mc** Michels	56 **Hi** Hill
49 10 **La** Laudrup	53 – **Lb** Lobanovskyi	57 **Bs** Bosman
50 10 **Bk** Bergkamp	54 – **Wg** Wenger	58 – **Av** Abramovich

51 –

Ch

Chapman

HERBERT CHAPMAN

(England, Manager)

The man who made the modern role of manager. Chapman had a modest playing career which ended at Northampton Town in the Southern League (then the third tier of English football), where he became player-manager in 1907, hanging up his boots two years later. As a straight manager, he enjoyed some success, leaving to take over at Leeds City for a couple of years before war broke out.

On the resumption of football after the First World War, Chapman found himself banned from the game as Leeds were thrown out of the league for making irregular payments: the ban was overturned with the help of Huddersfield Town, who wanted to employ Chapman. Football chairmen were a conservative breed in the main, but, at Huddersfield, Chapman found a board who supported his innovations. He employed a counter-attacking method that relied on superior fitness – he believed in clean lifestyles and rigorous self-discipline within his squad and a robust defence.

The half backs and inside forwards became less static than was the custom, and more akin to modern midfield players, while the wingers were encouraged to cut inside and join in play rather than hugging the touchline and waiting for the ball.

Chapman was also very specific in choosing players to suit his system. His captain at Huddersfield, Clem Stephenson, was reckoned to be coming to the end of his career when Chapman bought him, but Stephenson helped the club win a hat-trick of league titles in the 1920s before retiring at the end of the decade.

Another to benefit from Chapman's management was the winger Cliff Bastin at Arsenal. Chapman became manager of Arsenal in 1925 and signed Bastin in 1929: he possessed a fearsome shot and became a prolific goalscorer under Chapman, often netting as many in a season as the centre forward.

With both Huddersfield and Arsenal, Chapman was manager of two clubs that won three consecutive league titles: Huddersfield in the early twenties and Arsenal in the thirties, although he was in charge only for the first two in both cases.

He was poached by Arsenal, jealous of Huddersfield's success, and he tragically died mid-season while manager of Arsenal after contracting pneumonia.

Chapman was dogged by financial scandals and while at Arsenal he managed to avoid implication in a crisis involving illegal payments to club captain Charlie Buchan while the chairman was banned for life.

He was a man prepared to use any means at his disposal to get the upper hand but also one with a restless mind who liked tinkering and experimenting: he persuaded the authorities to rename Gillespie Road Underground as Arsenal to show off the club; he also introduced numbered shirts for his players and experimented with floodlit matches and training.

Chemical reaction: take one perceptive manager, add cash – result: trophies.

RINUS MICHELS

(Holland, Coach)

Rinus Michels played under the imaginative English coach Jack Reynolds at Ajax and was also an admirer of the fluid Hungarian team of the 1950s. It was inevitable that those strong influences would be absorbed into the way he asked his players to play at Ajax in the late 1960s.

The style became known as Total Football, a tactical system that has been misunderstood over the years like no other. There is a notion that the Ajax players (and those in the Dutch national side) switched positions at will to bamboozle the opposition. This simply wasn't the case: Ruud Krol, for example, was a left back, and he played at left back for the entire game, never popping up on the right wing or dictating play from central midfield while Johan Neeskens had a breather at full back. It meant that all the players were comfortable on the ball, and all of them were acutely aware of movement and creating space. The players who moved at will were the creative influences, especially Johan Cruyff, who used the holes created by the others to hurt the opposition and to take possession.

Michels's teams were both successful and enjoyable to watch – although like Barcelona and Spain in recent years, their endless possession was sometimes lacking in a sharp end product. He won the European Cup with Ajax in 1971 with the team winning the next two under his successor, Stefan Kovacs; managing the national side, he took Holland to the 1974 World Cup final. In a later spell with the Dutch team he won the 1988 European Championship. A pretty good CV, but the award of FIFA Coach of the Century in 1999 was more for Michels's sophisticated grasp of the importance of space on the pitch – a concept way beyond most coaching minds.

Total Football wasn't solely Michels's invention, and it wasn't as different as some make out, but it was a definite shift, a move towards the athletic, fluid game played today.

Chemical reaction: the addition of an open mind to a crop of great players (add a dash of Cruyff) will produce unexpected results.

VALERIY LOBANOVSKYI

(Ukraine, Coach)

A logical step on from Michels, Valeriy Lobanovskyi took the principles of Total Football into his time as coach of Dynamo Kiev and added a further ingredient: pressing.

The Soviet sides were nothing if not fit and Lobanovskyi worked out that it could be their competitive advantage and might compensate for a lack of outstanding match-winning stars. His Kiev side, which effectively became the Soviet team, were one of Europe's best: their display against Atlético Madrid to win the European Cup Winners' Cup in 1986 was sublime, with Madrid barely getting a kick. After some lean times in the 1990s, Lobanovskyi returned to Kiev and made them once again the pre-eminent side in their own country and a force in Europe. In 1999 in a Champions League semi-final they had Bayern Munich on the rack but conceded two late goals in a 3-3 draw and lost the return 1-0.

With the national team, Lobanovskyi struggled to find the right blend and resorted to picking almost his entire Kiev side: Spartak Moscow's excellent goalkeeper Rinat Dasayev and the Belorussian playmaker Sergei Aleinikov were the only non-Kiev regulars. They reached the last sixteen of the World Cup in 1986 when defensive vulnerability cost them in a 4-3 thriller against Belgium. At the 1988 European Championship they fared even better, brushing aside England and Italy on their way to the final before succumbing to the brilliance of Holland's Holy Trinity of Gullit, van Basten and Rijkaard.

Back to the pressing: Lobanovskyi worked out that his ultra-fit teams could afford to play at a high tempo for longer than most and could, therefore, expend energy in chasing the opposition in their own half rather than allowing them to work the ball forwards. As fitness, nutrition and conditioning improved this principle of defending from the front became the norm, but it was Lobanovskyi's hard-working, star-free teams that pioneered the approach.

Chemical reaction: the addition of extra oxygen through conditioning leads to greater collective purpose – how very Soviet!

54	−
Wg	
Wenger	

ARSÈNE WENGER

(France, Coach)

When Arsenal sacked Bruce Rioch after a disappointing season in 1995–6, no one expected the next appointment would be an unheard of Frenchman managing a club in the J-League in Japan. Apparently Glenn Hoddle played his part, recommending with some enthusiasm a coach he played under at Monaco when they won the French league in 1988.

There was little precedent for such a move at the time – overseas coaches had not enjoyed much success in Britain. But when Wenger arrived perceptions about foreign managers quickly changed. Over the next ten years he built a team that challenged Manchester United for the major honours in England. United edged the contest, but Arsenal's 'on' years were outstanding: they won the double in 1998 and 2002 and finished an entire Premier League season unbeaten in 2004, a quite phenomenal achievement.

It was done in the main with astute foreign imports. Wenger inherited a formidably sturdy defence (Adams and Co.) and Dennis Bergkamp, but needed more. He brought in Patrick Vieira to match Keane at United and added the pace of Overmars and the finishing of Nicolas Anelka (replaced after 1998 with Thierry Henry). Others were bought young and developed, like Cesc Fàbregas. It was a blueprint others would follow, despite accusations it had a negative effect on the development of young English players.

Wenger also paid great attention to diet, psychology and computerised statistics not yet the norm in England. It was a methodology that many of the better English managers adopted, notably Sam Allardyce and Steve McClaren.

Wenger's teams play excellent sophisticated, scientific football. They have fallen away in the last decade partly through having less cash to burn than Chelsea or the Manchester clubs, and partly through a blind spot regarding defensive players. You can't win the league with some of the central defenders Wenger has deployed and no top-quality replacement for Patrick Vieira. There are signs another really good team is emerging, this time with a core of young British players.

Chemical reaction: the addition of new and unfamiliar theories will always bring change.

Column 13

		59 6 **Wr** Wright
		60 7 **Jz** Jairzinho
51 – **Ch** Chapman	55 – **Rt** Rimet	61 10 **Km** Kempes
52 – **Mc** Michels	56 – **Hi** Hill	62 10 **Mt** Matthäus
53 – **Lb** Lobanovskyi	57 – **Bs** Bosman	63 3 **Rc** Carlos
54 – **Wg** Wenger	58 – **Av** Abramovich	64 8 **Gr** Gerrard

55	–
Rt	
Rimet	

JULES RIMET

(France, Administrator)

If Charles Alcock (see Rare Earth Metals) was the man behind organised professional football, then Jules Rimet can take the credit for the game's premier international competition.

Rimet was appointed President of FIFA in 1921 and under his leadership the organisation rapidly expanded its membership (from a paltry 12 when he took over, there are over 200 members today). The game's administrators had always been lukewarm about another international competition on top of the Olympics, which was run by FIFA. Increased professionalism – very much a no-no at the Olympics – and a well-attended Olympic football tournament in Paris in 1924 provoked a rethink. The first World Cups followed two years after the 1928 Olympics and have remained on that timing cycle ever since.

The pre-war tournaments were lacking in some of the big sides, but once football got under way again after the Second World War the tournament became what it was intended to be – the ultimate test of international teams. The Soviet Union prevented those in their fiefdom from taking part, but they all eventually returned during the fifties. The original World Cup trophy was renamed after Rimet, and was given to Brazil when they won their third tournament in 1970 (it has since been stolen, never to be seen again). Rimet himself was long gone by this time; he died in 1956 aged eighty-three, two years after relinquishing office as FIFA's longest serving President.

Chemical reaction: take Corinthian amateurism and professional football and you will find the two separate entirely.

56	–
Hi	
Hill	

JIMMY HILL

(England, Midfielder/Administrator/Coach/Commentator)

In his last years as a commentator on the BBC, Jimmy Hill became something of a figure of fun. His prominent chin and pointy beard and, at times, pompous delivery left him open to ridicule and mimicry. But this obscures the true nature of his contribution to the game.

Hill started playing at Brentford but his best playing days came in a decade at Fulham, from 1952 to 1961, where he was the prompter and brains of a team that included the divine skills of Johnny Haynes, the club's finest player.

While at Fulham, Hill became Chairman of the Professional Footballers' Association, a hitherto somewhat toothless players' union. Under his charge, the union fought and won George Eastham's claim against Newcastle for restraint of trade after they refused him a transfer – the Bosman ruling of its day (see below). He also fought a successful campaign to end the maximum wage ruling. I doubt Hill envisaged how much his laudable work would change the lifestyle of the professional footballer.

Hill became manager of Coventry City still aged only thirty-three and utterly transformed the club from a humdrum third-tier outfit into a team that enjoyed unbroken top-flight status from 1967 to 2001. He left the club, just as they were promoted, to pursue a media career.

He became Head of Sport at London Weekend Television for a while but moved to the BBC to front *Match of the Day* in 1973, becoming synonymous with the programme over the next twenty years: Hill's distinctive look, voice and mass of knowledge added a gravitas that no football programme had managed before. He had a further eight years presenting a football chat show on Sky before retiring in 2001 just short of his eightieth birthday. He even took over as chairman of Fulham at a parlous stage in the club's history and led them away from bankruptcy.

Hill is a true football polymath who has been a success in every aspect of the game.

Chemical reaction: sprinkle Jimmy Hill on a problem and you will get a clear solution.

JEAN-MARC BOSMAN

(Belgium, Midfielder)

An ordinary footballer who changed the face of the game, Bosman was playing for RFC Liège (not the better known Standard Liége) and saw out his contract in 1990. He wanted to move to Dunkerque in France but Liège wanted a fee so blocked the move. Bosman contested this and took it all the way to the European Court of Justice. The ruling was in his favour and henceforth clubs were no longer able to charge fees for players who had completed their contract (unless the player is under twenty-four, when a compensation for development clause comes in).

While the ruling was clearly correct and fair, the results have largely been negative. Smaller clubs have been unable to reap the rewards of hiring and developing players and selling them on. More freedom of movement has increased the influence of players' agents within the game and they have not been a force for good.

Chemical reaction: take two disaffected parties, add lawyers and put them all in court. The result? All the money will depart the disaffected parties and migrate towards the lawyers.

ROMAN ABRAMOVICH

(Russia, Chairman)

Roman Abramovich is here as representative of a breed: the celebrity chairman. Football is their playground, not their livelihood, but they wield enormous influence, not just on the club they control but on the game as a whole. Abramovich isn't the worst of the breed, or the best, or the first, and he certainly won't be the last but he is one of the more high profile and one whose presence had a profound effect on a particular club's fortunes.

When Abramovich bought Chelsea they were a decent club. They won the league in the 1950s and won the FA Cup three times. Since the oil magnate (and former rubber-duck vendor) took over in 2003 they have won both a further four times and also added a coveted Champions League title. Abramovich has hired and sacked some of the most high-profile coaches of his time with varying degrees of success: Avram Grant did okay but was dour and dull; 'Big Phil' Scolari was comically unsuited to working in England; Carlos Ancelotti won the double but failed in Europe; and André Villas-Boas was too inexperienced (it was the stand-in after he was sacked, Roberto Di Matteo, who led the club to their only Champions League triumph). Guus Hiddink and Rafa Benítez both had spells at the club, but only as stop-gaps.

Abramovich's best decision was undoubtedly the appointment of José Mourinho after the Portuguese won the Champions League with Porto in 2004.

Under 'The Special One' (Mourinho's own words), Chelsea won their first league title in fifty years and added another the following year. The Champions League eluded them and Mourinho left for Inter; Abramovich could only watch enviously as Mourinho won the Champions League with the Italian side.

Abramovich's second-best decision was rehiring Mourinho in 2013 – the league duly returned to Stamford Bridge during his second season back.

Abramovich attends most of Chelsea's games and is a genuine football fan who expects only success in return for his investment, not money back. He has transformed Chelsea into serial winners.

Elton John at Watford, Silvio Berlusconi at Milan, the Agnelli family at Juventus, Sheikh Mansour bin Zayed Al Nahyan at Manchester City – their stories are similar. Mike Ashley at Newcastle? He would be in a different section.

Chemical reaction: take one middling successful club; add cash until expansion and trophies ensue.

Porous

The players in this section are not rubbish, far from it. They are players who have won most things football has to offer between them; they have racked up international appearances and earned glowing reputations in the game.

They are also players who have been well served, flattered even, by commentators and the media to give us a sense that their value and contribution was greater than it actually was. The porous in their group name refers to reputation: pour on the cold water of deeper analysis and it doesn't hold.

Column 14

	59 6 **Wr** Wright	**65** 1 **Fk** Foulke
	60 7 **Jz** Jairzinho	**66** 7 **Ra** Rahn
55 – **Rt** Rimet	**61** 10 **Km** Kempes	**67** 6 **Bx** Baxter
56 – **Hi** Hill	**62** 10 **Mt** Matthäus	**68** 8 **Sc** Schuster
57 – **Bs** Bosman	**63** 3 **Rc** Carlos	**69** 10 **Bg** Baggio
58 – **Av** Abramovich	**64** 8 **Gr** Gerrard	**70** 8/10 **Sv** Stoichkov

59 6
Wr
Wright

BILLY WRIGHT

(England, Central Defender)

Billy Wright was a really good player, just not an all-time great. Wright played in an era when top-class English defenders were in short supply, as the heavy losses they received playing against Hungary in 1953 and again in 1954 testify. Harry Johnston was regarded as a good centre half until the Hungarians ran riot, and the much-vaunted Syd Owen played in sides that conceded twelve goals in his three caps.

Neil Franklin, England's first choice centre back after the war, played his last international game in 1950 and was, arguably, never adequately replaced. While this is not explicitly Wright's fault, he was the team captain, and the defensive half back, and must bear some responsibility for England's failure to counter not just the Hungarians but opponents in the World Cup tournaments of 1954 and 1958.

Wright was a rigid player (they were rigid times). He needed the discipline of a strict formation, such as he enjoyed at Wolverhampton under Stan Cullis, and he lacked the sophistication to adapt his game to the more technical arena of the international game. He wasn't alone as there was a general inability to adapt across the board in British football at this time.

Wright's glowing reputation is based on being the first player to receive 100 international caps – a spectacular achievement – not on his brilliance as a player. Ahmed Hassan won 184 caps for Egypt and that doesn't mean he was a world-class player either.

Conclusion: if your team loses 7-1 and you are a defender, you haven't done well.

JAIRZINHO

(Brazil, Winger)

Jairzinho was scintillating in Brazil's 1970 World Cup campaign. He scored in every round and looked to be a threat every time he got the ball. Mind you, so did all of his colleagues. He was quick and direct and had a rasping shot in his right boot. But when he had to play on the other side of the pitch to accommodate Garrincha at the start of his international career he struggled to make an impact.

In 1970, though, Jairzinho was at his peak. The service he received was of the highest class: slide-rule passes inside the full back from Gerson and Pelé and great hold-up play from Tostão were the stuff of dreams for an instinctive player. He scored against the Czechs and Romania – hard working but unremarkable sides – and scored the only goal of the game against a strong England defence. Crucially this gave Brazil the soft side of the draw and they easily disposed of Peru (gifted but lightweight at the back) and Uruguay (who took the lead but then hardly had a kick). In the final, Italy were surprisingly compliant, perhaps exhausted after a brutal 120 minutes against West Germany. Jairzinho's seventy-first minute goal, Brazil's third, ensured he became the first player since Alcides Ghiggia in 1950 to score in every round of a World Cup Finals tournament. He remains the last.

Four years later Jairzinho was back, but in an inferior and curiously defensive Brazil team. The team got past some modest opposition but were exposed when they met the Dutch, who inflicted one of the easiest World Cup defeats (2-0) on a Brazilian side until the debacle of 2014.

Jairzinho was flattered by his teammates in 1970. In Brazilian terms he was an also-ran, some way short of the top level. Unlike Didi, Garrincha, Pelé, Zico, Romário, Rivaldo, Ronaldo, Neymar and all those other genius-level players Brazil has produced, he couldn't raise his team up when they were struggling: he was never the go-to guy.

Conclusion: one swallow does not a summer make.

MARIO KEMPES

(Argentina, Forward)

Kempes had a good career with Valencia in Spain, winning the *Copa del Rey* and the European Cup Winners' Cup. He was *La Liga* top scorer for a couple of years going into the 1978 World Cup tournament, where he was César Luis Menotti's only foreign-based pick for the Argentina side. Kempes was a revelation: big and strong but athletic, he bullied the weaker defences and troubled the stronger ones.

In the first phase of the competition Kempes played second fiddle to Leopoldo Luque, but when the River Plate man was injured he took centre stage, scoring twice against Poland in the second group phase and adding another brace of goals against Peru (Argentina won 6-0 to take them through to the final on goal difference at the expense of Brazil). He was terrific in the final against Holland, scoring twice and tormenting the experienced Dutch defence.

So why is he in the Porous category?

Kempes also played in the 1974 finals and looked lost – we'll excuse him that, he was still a teenager. But he also returned in 1982 and played in a team that included the boy wonder Maradona. Again he scored no goals and was a dead loss. The conclusion has to be that this was a good player who enjoyed an outstanding tournament in 1978. Yes, he did well in Spain, but *La Liga* was at a low ebb and he was never tested in *Serie A* or the English First Division, both much stronger leagues at the time.

Conclusion: the one swallow... thing again.

LOTHAR MATTHÄUS

(Germany, Midfielder)

There was definitely something unlovable about the German team of the late eighties and early nineties. *Tor!*, the brilliant book about German football by Ulrich Hesse-Lichtenberger, concedes this very fact. The sides that won the World Cup in 1954, 1974 and 2014 are the stuff of legend: the side that won in 1990 was a bit... well... just... *yeah*. They were also a bit *too* full or arrogance and inflated self-belief. When Germany lost unexpectedly to Bulgaria at the next World Cup in 1994, there was a delectable shudder of *schadenfreude* throughout the footballing world.

Matthäus won a lot of trophies, and was a key player for West Germany and Germany over two decades, including twenty-five appearances in five World Cup tournaments, a record that is unlikely to be beaten. He was strong and purposeful, really fit and aggressive with a powerful shot and rarely got injured (hence the 150 caps), but there was something a bit mechanical about his game: he provided drive and thrust but relied on others for the magic. Matthäus clearly had an iron will, though, because he led Germany to victories in numerous games where they were outplayed.

In his later years when the legs had gone he moved into defence. To the relief of many he was slow and ineffectual in the new role.

Matthäus was a good player, but not a true great.

Conclusion: if nobody sings your praises outside your Wikipedia page there is probably a reason.

ROBERTO CARLOS

(Brazil, Left Back)

Is it a bit strong to suggest Roberto Carlos was rubbish and that Brazil and Real Madrid won in spite of him at left back instead of because of it? Probably.

At the same time, he appeared to give away possession more than anyone else on his team by being too ambitious or over-elaborate. For every one of the few spectacular free kicks he got on target, he blasted any number into Row Z, often shooting from preposterous range and angles. You could see goalkeepers look fidgety and jittery if Zidane or Figo or Beckham stood over a free kick, but not if it was Carlos: they knew the percentages were in their favour.

Roberto Carlos was quick, strong and aggressive. He could pass, go past a man and cross reasonably well. He should have been the perfect full back, not a defensive liability as he was, for example, in the 2006 World Cup quarter-final between Brazil and France. It was not a vintage Brazilian team, but Lúcio was marshalling the defence expertly and even an overweight Ronaldo offered the threat of a goal on the counter. Then France got a free kick on the left, which Zidane hit hard and high beyond the main group of French attackers. They were the decoy because Zidane and Thierry Henry had noticed that Roberto Carlos was re-tying his laces. The ball dropped into a wide-open space for Henry to volley past a hapless goalkeeper. On the TV footage, Carlos is not even on screen when his man scores the game's only goal. One moment, but it encapsulates this monstrously overrated player.

Conclusion: show enough plumage and no one will notice the lack of meat.

STEVEN GERRARD

(England, Midfielder)

The 2005 Champions League final between Liverpool and AC Milan was an epic affair. In the first half Liverpool were embarrassing, and extremely lucky to only be three down at half time after being cut apart by Andrea Pirlo's passing and the movement of Kaká, Hernán Crespo and

Andriy Shevchenko. Harry Kewell had proved a dreadful and erroneous gamble by Rafa Benítez, and his system was exposed as naive and porous. At half time Benítez brought on Didi Hamann (who should have started). It was hardly a masterplan but it worked. Gerrard pushed Milan on to the back foot, scoring a goal to give Liverpool hope and winning the penalty that brought them parity. He did exactly the same when his side were struggling the following year in the FA Cup final against West Ham.

Gerrard had everything. He could tackle, sprint, head the ball, pass long or short and score goals, and in these games he showed his full repertoire. But he just didn't do it often enough, especially for England. Gerrard had loads of good games for his country, but rarely did he look the dominant game-changer he could be for Liverpool. And none of his managers at international level solved the conundrum of how to play Gerrard and Frank Lampard in the same team. (One player was noted for their accurate long passes, the other a noted goalscorer with a knack for being in the penalty area at the right time – which would you make play deeper?)

Gerrard deserved all the accolades he received in 2015 at the end of his Liverpool career, but the ending of his England career, a limp exit from the 2014 World Cup, was equally appropriate – even if, belatedly, he performed well in a deeper role.

A top player and a nice man, but he belongs in the 'also starring' part of the cast list.

Conclusion: history can be, and will be, a harsh judge.

Unpredictables

Expect the unexpected. That's what the Unpredictables bring to a team, for good or ill. These players, incendiary on their good days, had a few bad ones when their colleagues might as well have played without them. These are not the-perfect-role-model sort of players; they are the ones picked for their massive talent in the hope that today is one of the days they might display it.

There are various reasons for the unpredictability of these players. Some liked a drink and it showed sometimes while others were simply unable to muster their A-game on occasions. And some, like William Foulke, were like cartoon characters.

Column 15

71	9
Le	
Leônidas	

59	6	65	1	72	10
Wr		**Fk**		**Ps**	
Wright		Foulke		PuskáS	

60	7	66	7	73	13
Jz		**Ra**		**Ft**	
Jairzinho		Rahn		Fontaine	

61	10	67	6	74	13
Km		**Bx**		**Gm**	
Kempes		Baxter		Müller	

62	10	68	8	75	10
Mt		**Sc**		**Ma**	
Matthäus		Schuster		Maradona	

63	3	69	10	76	9
Rc		**Bg**		**Ro**	
Carlos		Baggio		Ronaldo	

64	8	70	8/10	77	7
Gr		**Sv**		**Cr**	
Gerrard		Stoichkov		Cr Ronaldo	

65	1
Fk	
Foulke	

WILLIAM FOULKE

(England, Goalkeeper)

One of the first great characters of professional football, William Foulke was a goalkeeper for Sheffield United around the turn of the last century. In those less PC days he earned the soubriquet 'Fatty' – not much working out to do there about his nickname.

Foulke made his debut for the Blades aged twenty in 1894 and enjoyed eleven successful years at Bramall Lane, winning a league title in 1898 as well as his solitary England cap. He was a big lad, but reckoned to be still very agile for his size.

As he grew older, he grew larger. It is alleged that the terrace chant 'Who ate all the pies?' was first aimed at Foulke, who by the time he left for Chelsea for a then-handsome £20 fee was weighing-in close to twenty stone (around 150 kg). It is on record in the local Sheffield newspaper that Foulke's habit of swinging his vast bulk from the crossbar led to the demise of more than one set of goalposts.

Foulke is credited with the invention of ball boys after hiring a couple of kids while at Chelsea to stand behind the goal and try and put off the opposing forwards. They would often fetch the ball when it went behind to speed up play.

More than one forward paid for their temerity in shoulder charging him – Liverpool were once awarded a penalty when Foulke allegedly picked up their centre forward George Allan by one leg and dropped him on his head. It was legal and quite common to barge the goalkeeper into the goal off the shoulder – it happened less to Foulke than many other goalkeepers. He had a temper too. At the end of the drawn 1902 FA Cup final he supposedly chased the referee out of his changing room and into a broom cupboard. Foulke was entirely naked at the time. While not the greatest goalkeeper ever seen, he was one of the most entertaining and memorable.

Foulke + pies = no pies.

HELMUT RAHN

(Germany, Winger)

Helmut Rahn played for Rot-Weiss Essen, the unfashionable club from the North Rhine. You had to be pretty good to be picked for the national team if you played for Essen, and Rahn was. He was built like a barrel, had a mean gear change and a cannon of a right foot – strange, then, that he scored his most famous goal with his left. When not in the mood, he could be truly awful, wasteful in possession and lacklustre. But to get his good days, his moods were worth the bother.

Rahn was left out of the original West German squad for the 1954 World Cup Finals after a less than inspiring season, but showed great form on a tour of South America and so was brought to Switzerland by Sepp Herberger. Rahn played only once in the group stage, during which West Germany endured an 8-3 thrashing from Hungary, but he played well and Herberger used him in the latter stages. In the final, also against Hungary, Rahn scored the equaliser and then the winner deep into the second half, surprising Hungarian left back Mihály Lantos by cutting inside and shooting with his left foot.

Rahn liked to drink and was out of shape a few years later, but stern words from Herberger caught him just in time and he put in another sterling shift in a much weaker side at the 1958 World Cup in Sweden.

At home Rahn helped Essen win their only major title, the *DFB-Pokal* (German Cup) in 1953 – he scored the second, winning goal against equally unfashionable Aachen. Fifty years after the Miracle of Bern a statue was erected outside the Essen stadium to the town's most famous sporting hero.

Nickname: Der Boss. Why a disobedient maverick would earn this soubriquet it not clear. Arguably, Fritz Walter was the boss of the West German team in the 1950s.

67	6
Bx	
Baxter	

JIM BAXTER

(Scotland, Midfielder/Playmaker)

When Baxter was at Sunderland in the mid-sixties he was reputed to drink until he couldn't stand on a Friday and then turn up and play like a God on Saturday afternoon.

Baxter was at Sunderland because Rangers got fed up with his attitude and his boozing. Soon Sunderland moved him on to Nottingham Forest and he managed a last hurrah back at Rangers before retiring at thirty-one. He only lived to sixty-one, dying of pancreatic cancer and after receiving two liver transplants in his fifties.

Baxter won three Scottish league titles at Rangers, and during the 1960s he was an integral part of a Scotland team. In 1963, Baxter scored twice in a 2-1 win against England (with ten men after a serious injury to full back Eric Caldow). Scotland defeated England again in 1967 giving them a half-serious claim to being the world's best team after beating the now World Cup holders 3-2. The game is remembered for Baxter playing 'keepy-uppy' with the ball while waiting for teammates to find space. These sixties teams were probably the best Scotland ever fielded: Baxter, Denis Law, Dave Mackay, Jimmy Johnstone – these were all top notch players.

Left-footed, Baxter had near perfect balance and seemed to have all the time in the world to play his passes. He could beat a man with a sashay worthy of a ballroom champion and his touch and footwork were impeccable. On his game, he was arguably the best player ever to pull on the blue jersey of Scotland. But he had off days, and too many of them.

Nickname: Slim Jim. A largely liquid diet and rigorous exercise will keep the body lean.

BERND SCHUSTER

(West Germany, Midfielder)

Never heard of him? You're not alone: he is the forgotten genius of German football. At the 1980 European Championship a pedestrian West Germany side won the competition in spite of a lack of world-beaters. Their best players were all at the fledgling stage of their career: at the back was the aggressive centre half Karl-Heinz Förster; up front was striker Karl-Heinz Rummenigge; and in midfield, the man dictating play was Bernd Schuster.

Schuster soon acquired a reputation as one of the best midfield players in the world, even at twenty. He was fast and powerful, with two feet and a ripper of a shot – the ideal attacking midfield player. He made his name at Cologne, but signed for Barcelona in 1980, becoming the mainstay of the Catalan giants for most of the next decade, recovering well after a typically dangerous tackle from the 'Butcher of Bilbao', Andoni Goikoetxea.

This wasn't the multi-talented Barcelona of recent years and they were lean years for the club. Between 1960 and 1990 Barça won only two titles, one in 1974 and one in 1985, when Schuster drove them to the top. The club's leading scorer was ex-Tottenham striker Steve Archibald, hardly a name to strike fear into Europe's best defenders, but when Schuster was on his game there were plenty of chances to feed off.

So why only twenty-two caps for West Germany? The man could be obstreperous and stubborn. He refused to attend player socials, he missed an international game to be at the birth of his son, which was unacceptable in the eighties, and some argue that his wife, who also acted as his agent, put some noses out of joint. Eventually, his relationship with manager Jupp Derwall deteriorated and Schuster quit playing for West Germany at the age of twenty-four.

Nickname: The Blond Angel.

69   10

Bg

Baggio

ROBERTO BAGGIO

(Italy, Forward)

It was easy to wonder what the fuss was about with Roberto Baggio on the occasions when he plodded around the pitch and struggled to get into the game. Yet he had a fantastic reputation in Italy where he was loved at all the clubs he played for – which included Fiorentina, Juventus, Milan, Bologna and Inter. Indeed, there was local upset when he left Fiorentina to join Juventus for a then world record transfer fee of £8 million. He never celebrated scoring against his old team and once refused to take a penalty against them, claiming they knew where he would put it.

Baggio scored twenty-seven goals in fifty-six games for Italy. He would have played a lot more had he not fallen out with Arrigo Sacchi in the mid-nineties and only played three games between 1995 and 1997. Which was a shame, because these may have been his best years, as shown by his performances at the 1994 World Cup Finals. Italy were dire in the group phase and only crept through to the knockout stages; in the second game against Norway, Baggio suffered the ignominy of being the player sacrificed when the goalkeeper Gianluca Pagliuca was dismissed and a replacement brought on.

Despite this, when Italy were losing in their last-sixteen match against Nigeria, Sacchi stuck with Baggio – and just as well. He intervened with a late equaliser and added the winning spot kick in extra time. In the quarter-final he repeated the trick, applying a super-cool finish to an Italian break to beat Spain in the dying minutes. In the semi-final against Bulgaria, Baggio scored another two goals: the first a scintillating turn and dribble followed by a wonderfully executed, curling daisy cutter.

No happy ending: the abiding image of that moribund tournament is Baggio hanging his head after missing a penalty in the final shoot out against Brazil. Harsh – he was the tournament's best player.

Nickname: The Divine Ponytail. Perhaps it's cooler in Italian *(Il Divino Codino)*.

HRISTO STOICHKOV

70	8/10
Sv	
Stoichkov	

(Bulgaria, Forward)

It was a 1994 World Cup quarter-final and Germany were hot favourites. If there was a doubt they would win it was down to how their creaky defence would cope with Hristo Stoichkov, the Barcelona forward who was so instrumental in the rise of Johan Cruyff's Catalan side.

Stoichkov was a left-footed player, but Cruyff allowed him freedom to roam. He would do as much damage cutting in from the right or slipping deep to unleash his formidable shooting power as he would in a conventional left-sided role. On the down side he earned too many yellow and red cards, often for arguing with the referee.

He had been the best player at his previous club, CSKA Sofia, and it was debatable how he would fit in with the other Barcelona superstars. Cruyff had the knack of getting something out of the fractious Bulgarian. There were off days, and sent-off days, but in the main Stoichkov played nicely with Laudrup and Romário.

Back to 1994 and Germany took the lead when a typically preposterous Klinsmann dive earned a penalty, taken by Lothar Matthäus. The expressions on the German faces were easily readable – the result seemed done and dusted.

When Stoichkov matched Klinsmann's theatrics at the other end of the pitch, however, the referee awarded Bulgaria a soft free kick. Stoichkov was a dead eye from twenty to thirty yards out and he bent a perfect shot into the huge space Bodo Illgner had left in the corner of his goal. Minutes later Zlatko Yankov dinked an innocuous cross into the area followed by Yordan Letchkov, who gave away the earlier penalty, powering a header into the top corner.

It was Bulgaria's best day – they lost the semi-final to Italy – but Stoichkov was to have other magic moments: five *La Liga* titles and a European Cup with Barcelona, where he remains a bona fide legend.

Nickname: *El Pistolero* (The Gunslinger) on account of his ferocious and occasionally indiscriminate shooting.

Explosives

Some players work hard throughout a game and make a positive but unobtrusive contribution. There's nothing extravagant about Nemanja Vidić, Clarence Seedorf or Miroslav Klose: they just make sure they are in the right place at the right time. Sometimes, decision making is just as important a factor in their game as extravagant gifts.

Others players, however, including all those in this group in our table, eschew the safety of the simple pass. They like to take players on with searing pace or intricate skills; rather than lay the ball off with their chest, they will attempt an overhead kick. These players are often quiet for much of a game, waking up to interject their unique skills and change the course of the play. They are often explosive: light the touchpaper and stand clear.

Column 16

71 9 **Le** Leônidas	78 9 **Si** Sindelar

65 1 **Fk** Foulke	72 10 **Ps** PuskáS	79 7 **Ga** Garrincha
66 7 **Ra** Rahn	73 13 **Ft** Fontaine	80 7 **Be** Best
67 6 **Bx** Baxter	74 13 **Gm** Müller	81 19 **Gz** Gascoigne
68 8 **Sc** Schuster	75 10 **Ma** Maradona	82 7 **Ca** Cantona
69 10 **Bg** Baggio	76 9 **Ro** Ronaldo	83 16 **Ke** Keane
70 8/10 **Sv** Stoichkov	77 7 **Cr** Cr Ronaldo	84 10 **Zd** Zidane

71	9
Le	
Leônidas	

LEÔNIDAS

(Brazil, Forward)

The Brazilian team that travelled to France to compete in the 1938 World Cup had two bona fide superstars: one was Domingos da Guia, the centre-half and playmaker, the other Leônidas, the main striker and goalscorer. Both played for the Flamengo club in Rio, having returned to Brazil after spells in Uruguay. Leônidas was one of only a handful of black players to earn selection for Flamengo.

Brazilian football before the war (and for some time after) was dominated by the European ex-pats, and the black players were treated very much as second-class citizens, having to work harder to earn recognition than their white peers.

Europe had a brief glimpse of Leônidas in the previous World Cup in Italy when he scored Brazil's only goal in a 3-1 first-round defeat against Spain. Four years later, he still had the same elastic athleticism but had added more polish and composure in front of goal.

Most of the potted biographies concentrate on his pioneering use of the overhead kick: no one can truly say who was the first to try an acrobatic aerial volley, but it was certainly part of Leônidas's armoury. It is highly likely that opposing defenders were often grateful to see the ball ballooned into Row Z instead of being headed neatly into the corner, the efficacy of such tricks being often overstated.

Leônidas's pace and power brought him seven goals in the 1938 tournament and who knows how many more he might have scored had the Second World War not interfered with his international career. After scoring a hat-trick against Poland and in both the quarter-final and replay against Czechoslovakia, Leônidas was left out of the team for the semi-final against Italy. Reports suggest he was tired after the replay and being rested for the final; if true, this was a catastrophic error. Brazil were beaten 2-1 and Leônidas lost his last chance at World Cup glory.

He earns his place in football history, not for a few spectacular overhead kicks, but for being the first black Brazilian player to make himself an international star and show the way forward for the next, staggeringly talented generation.

Leônidas + acrobatics = 2% goal chance.

72   10

Ps

Puskás

FERENC PUSKÁS

(Hungary, Forward)

It's Wednesday 25 November 1953 and England and Hungary take the field at Wembley in front of a packed house for the year's most eagerly awaited international friendly. Hungary were the Olympic champions while England carried the title of Europe's best team and had never been beaten at home against sides from outside the United Kingdom.

The assumption of superiority from the home side and their supporters was evident in the tittering of the crowd at the sight of the slightly portly, bow-legged Hungarian number ten. This was one of the most feared strikers in Europe? Really?

Two hours later, no one questioned Hungary's supremacy, and no one questioned the brilliance of their number ten. Ferenc Puskás's delicate touch, movement and surprising turn of speed bamboozled the English defence as much as the team's sophisticated tactics and passing as a whole. Puskás only ever seemed to use his left foot but it didn't matter; one is enough when the foot in question is as accurate and explosive as Puskás's left.

Puskás should have ended up a World Cup winner the following year. He scored the opening goal in the final as Hungary took a 2-0 lead, but a hairline fracture reduced his contribution. The redoubtable West German team refused to submit and came back to snatch the trophy. It was the last time Hungary made a significant contribution to a major finals tournament. Before qualification for the next World Cup came around Soviet tanks rolled into Budapest and a number of key players defected to the West, Puskás among them. Most of his team, Honvéd, refused to return to Budapest after the second leg of their European Cup tie against Athletic Bilbao, which was played on neutral territory in Brussels.

After serving a two-year ban imposed by UEFA on all the Hungarian ex-pats who fled the country after the Soviet invasion Puskás was offered a contract by Real Madrid in 1958. He was thirty-one, and Real were taking a bit of a risk, but they were repaid in spades. The Spanish giants dominated *La Liga* and the European Cup for the next few years and Puskás hit the net at almost a goal a game for another six years. He scored four goals in Real's remarkable win over Eintracht Frankfurt in the 1960 European Cup final, and another final hat-trick, this time in defeat, as Real lost the 1962 final 5-3 to Benfica. Puskás did appear in the World Cup Finals tournament again, for Spain in 1962, but his potency at that level had diminished. It is for his performances for Hungary in the early 1950s, and his goalscoring for Real Madrid that he will be remembered; and for that vicious left foot.

Puskás earned the nickname the Galloping Major: slightly inappropriate, as he was only a Lieutenant in the army (an honorary title).

73   13
Ft
Fontaine

JUST FONTAINE

(France, Forward)

In 1958 Just Fontaine scored thirteen goals in one World Cup Finals tournament, a record that is unlikely to be broken. Drafted into the starting eleven at the last minute, Fontaine, a prolific scorer with the successful Reims side, kicked off the campaign with a hat-trick as France hammered Paraguay. He scored two more goals against Yugoslavia, although this game ended in defeat for France, and one more in a win against Scotland, which took his tally to six in the group matches. Contemporary reports talk of the Moroccan-born striker's blistering pace and most of his goals came from through balls or accelerating past defenders onto crosses.

Fontaine scored two more goals against Northern Ireland – tired after a post-group play-off – in the quarter-finals. In an entertaining semi-final, which Brazil won 5-2, he scored again. During the third-place match, where France beat West Germany 6-3, Fontaine scored another four times.

For a while Fontaine's reputation suffered and he was dismissed as a one-tournament wonder, but had his career not been beset by injuries after the tournament (he retired in 1962, still only twenty-eight) he could have achieved much more. It should be remembered France's appearance in the World Cup semi-finals was something of a surprise. They were not expected to go that far and that they did was largely down to the clinical finishing of Just Fontaine.

Fontaine was top scorer in the following season's European Cup too, but couldn't find the net in the final against Real Madrid. Reims lost 2-0.

GERD MÜLLER

(West Germany, Forward)

Known as *Der Bomber*, Müller was the most lethal finisher the game has seen. Gerd Müller scored sixty-eight goals in sixty-two international matches and nearly a goal a game in over five hundred games for Bayern Munich (after a single prolific teenage season at 1861 Nördlingen). The international figure is remarkable: West Germany rarely wasted time with friendlies in the sixties and seventies, meaning that Müller's goals were scored mainly in qualifiers, final tournaments and games against other top teams. He played thirteen games in the World Cup Finals and scored fourteen times, including successive hat-tricks in 1970 and the winning goal in the

1974 final against Holland. He added another four as West Germany won the 1972 European Championship.

Müller won four *Bundesliga* titles and played in all three of Bayern's successive European Cup victories in 1974, 1975 and 1976, scoring in two of them. He retired from international football while only twenty-eight after the 1974 World Cup, but carried on scoring goals for Bayern until 1979, when he headed to the US for a well-earned final payday.

Müller had short legs and a stocky frame. He didn't look much but his stature gave him exquisite balance and his powerful upper body carried him past players with strength as much as skill. He could finish with either foot and with his head. Müller held the record of most goals in a calendar year until it was broken by Lionel Messi – although Messi got a few more easy ones against inferior teams in the unbalanced Spanish league.

It was Müller who broke English hearts with West Germany's win in the quarter-final of the 1970 World Cup. England went with a better side than the one that won in 1966 and were 2-0 up after an outstanding hour.

DIEGO MARADONA

(Argentina, Attacking Midfielder)

Such is the strange make-up of this footballing talent that Diego Maradona could fit in a number of these groupings. For years Maradona was both bedrock and conductor of the Argentina team – if he turned up fit and played well, so did they. He was explosive and combustible, a man whose raw emotions were never far beneath the surface. He was certainly unpredictable and could be corrosive at times.

Maradona's seven years at Napoli brought them their only *Serie A* titles (1987 and 1990) and no single player, not even Pelé, has swayed a World Cup the way

Maradona dictated the 1986 tournament. Leading an otherwise ordinary side he added a layer of energy, and a ladleful of genius that saw them storm to the tournament. His cheating in the quarter-finals rankles with England fans but his performances in the knockout rounds were extraordinary. He tormented two strong defences (England and Belgium) with a series of cavalry-charge dribbles that had experienced international defenders flailing at thin air. Even in the final where he was less overtly effective, he dictated the pattern of the match as the Germans sacrificed their normal game to try and subdue him.

There were plenty of less savoury incidents too, including being thrown out of the 1994 World Cup after failing a drug test, starting a twenty-two-man brawl at the Spanish cup final in 1984 and threatening to shoot journalists who criticised him while manager of the national team. If it weren't for these personal flaws he would be one of football's most precious metals.

Maradona excused his cheating in 1986 by claiming his first goal was guided by 'the hand of God'. He did later accept that it was an illegal goal. Much frustration was aimed at the inexperienced referee – he called it wrong, but even with the TV cameras it wasn't immediately obvious what had happened.

RONALDO

(Brazil, Forward)

There were times in his career when Ronaldo looked as though he needed to spend more time in the gym – he turned up to the 2002 World Cup, for example, looking distinctly out of shape after an injury. Yet it never seemed to stop him scoring: even in that 2002 tournament he noticeably sharpened up throughout the competition and ended it the star turn and top scorer. His fifteen World Cup goals remained a record until eclipsed by Germany's Miroslav Klose in 2014.

Brazil won in 2002 and the previous tournament looked like ending with the same outcome until Ronaldo's mysterious seizure on the morning of the final. There was a 'will-he-won't-he' saga as the kick off approached as to whether he would play, and eventually Ronaldo took the field. He probably shouldn't have, he made no impact and Brazil lost.

After starting his club career in Europe in the relatively low-key environs of Eindhoven (where he formed a teenage partnership of rare talent with Eidur Gudjohnsen), Ronaldo moved to Bobby Robson's Barcelona where he was an instant hit. Spells at Inter Milan and Real Madrid proved he could score goals in the toughest leagues under the severest scrutiny. This was hardly surprising as he was truly gifted; quick, strong, with superb close control and unafraid to use either foot. Old Trafford doesn't often rise to salute an opponent but they did after Ronaldo scored a stunning hat-trick in a Champions League match in 2003.

Persistent injuries and recurring weight problems meant Ronaldo was finished as an international in 2006, aged just thirty (excepting for one ceremonial cap in 2011). He carried on scoring at club level when he was fit, even without the extra yard of pace that made him so special.

Ronaldo was an amiable character and great entertainer, both on the pitch and off. The media had great fun with his colourful love life. Explosive indeed.

Ronaldo is Brazil's second highest scorer after Pelé, with sixty-two goals in ninety-eight games, seven ahead of Romário, his predecessor. Both of them could be overtaken by Neymar, who is on forty-four and still only twenty-three.

77	7
Cr	
Cr Ronaldo	

CRISTIANO RONALDO

(Portugal, Forward)

The second best attacking player of the last decade, Cristiano Ronaldo has similar stats to his great rival,

Lionel Messi. Both score on average a goal a game in *La Liga* and both are talismanic and essential to their team's success. Ronaldo is more powerful and direct and a real threat in the air, while Messi is more intricate and a better team player. Both are deadly at set pieces. Neither has been able to muster his very best at a major international tournament.

Alex Ferguson's scouting team picked up Ronaldo after one hugely promising season for Sporting Lisbon. He wasn't an immediate success – his talent and power earned plaudits but he was inconsistent and given to excessive flamboyance and crowd-pleasing. Only in 2006–7, in the face of press and fan hostility after the 2006 European Championship (where he played a part in Wayne Rooney's red card), did Ronaldo blossom, finally scoring the 'ugly' goals his manager demanded as well as some poetic ones. Two more fine seasons led to a world-record transfer to Real Madrid (£80 million) while Ronaldo was still only twenty-four.

That is a phenomenal amount of money, but in the context of inflated finances in football, it was money well spent. Madrid finally wrestled the league back after a hat-trick of Barcelona wins and gained their coveted tenth Champions League title by beating Atlético Madrid in 2014, twelve years after the first *galácticos* side had won it for the ninth time. Ronaldo ended 2014–15 as Europe's top scorer again, for a record fourth time.

Putting aside a couple of stupid comments when he was younger, Ronaldo has a pretty clean public profile, and seems to have a good handle on what he wants.

Whither next? There seems to be little more he can do at Real and Portugal are declining, not improving. Cristiano Ronaldo could be what Major League Soccer in the US needs right now.

Combustibles

Every football fan likes a bit of drama. We look at the team sheets and see a couple of guys with a short fuse in opposition and we rub our hands in expectation of a few fireworks. Here is a collection of those players, the ones just as likely to change a game by seeing red as by scoring.

They are an essential part of the chemistry of any sport. Björn Borg would have been really dull if he hadn't had his rivalry with the tempestuous and ill-behaved John McEnroe; Ian Botham's 1981 heroics were so much more enjoyable knowing this was a man who had the stuffed shirts at the MCC tutting into their gin and tonics.

Column 17

		85 – **Bt** Blatter
71 9 **Le** Leônidas	78 9 **Si** Sindelar	86 – **Hv** Havelange
72 10 **Ps** PuskáS	79 7 **Ga** Garrincha	87 – **He** Herrera
73 13 **Ft** Fontaine	80 7 **Be** Best	88 5/10 **Rt** Rattín
74 13 **Gm** Müller	81 19 **Gz** Gascoigne	89 20 **Ro** Rossi
75 10 **Ma** Maradona	82 7 **Ca** Cantona	90 10 **Ln** Lentini
76 9 **Ro** Ronaldo	83 16 **Ke** Keane	91 – **Mu** Murdoch
77 7 **Cr** Cr Ronaldo	84 10 **Zd** Zidane	92 7/9 **Su** Suárez

MATTHIAS SINDELAR

(Austria, Playmaker)

It probably makes surprising reading for younger fans who are used to a handful of sides dominating every competition, but in the days between the two world wars, the most consistent team in Europe was Austria.

They were known as *Das Wunderteam* and enjoyed some famous victories under their astute coach Hugo Meisl (see Conductors). This included a 5-0 thrashing of a strong Scotland side in 1930 and an 8-2 victory against Hungary, no mean side themselves in the interwar years. Austria had good strikers in Johann Horvath, Josef Bican and Anton Schall, and a terrific playmaker in the skeletal figure of Matthias Sindelar, known as the Paper Man for his lack of physical presence. Sindelar was a ball-carrier with a knack of releasing the ball just as a tackle came, leaving the defender flailing at thin air. Austria went toe-to-toe with eventual winners Italy at the 1934 World Cup, losing their semi-final 1-0 in Milan.

It all came to an end when Adolf Hitler annex Austria in 1938. To 'celebrate' the *Anschluss*, a friendly was arranged between the German team, improving fast under Sepp Herberger, and the now-ageing 'old Austria' side. Sindelar gave the German opposition a masterclass. He was in his mid-thirties and had already indicated that he had no appetite for playing for a united Germano-Austrian side: he ran this game in his unique sinewy way, and often seemed to be taunting the Germans. When he scored the opening goal (after Austria missed a host of chances) he capered in front of the Nazi Party officials sitting in the stands.

Sindelar retired from football and bought a café from a Jewish friend in Vienna who was forced into exile. His sympathies were noted by the Party. Early the following year Sindelar and his girlfriend were found dead, supposedly from gas poisoning. The truth has never emerged but few believed the official version.

Ignition key: show him a swastika and enjoy the antics.

GARRINCHA

(Brazil, Winger)

When Pelé was injured in the second game of the 1962 World Cup Finals tournament, it left Brazil without their best player and talisman. They got lucky in two respects: firstly, the tournament was of poor quality with a lack of formidable teams; and secondly, another Brazilian emerged as the competition's star performer.

Manuel Francisco Dos Santos, better known as Garrincha, chose the latter stages of the tournament to show his full potential. The tricky little winger with the lurching gait – he had one leg shorter than the other after a childhood illness – made his Brazilian debut in 1955, and was in the side which won the World Cup in Sweden in 1958. Initially, Garrincha was viewed with suspicion by the management team and authorities because he lived out the cliché of the Brazilian street kid thrown into the professional game, often showing off and teasing opponents as if he were enjoying a kick about on the beach with his mates. Crowds loved him, but he could be frustrating for teammates and coaches.

In the 1962 quarter-final he tormented the England defence, scoring two goals in a 3-1 win against arguably the strongest side left in the tournament. Another two goals against hosts Chile and Brazil were in the final. Garrincha ought to have missed the final – he was sent off in the latter stages of the game against Chile – but some negotiation (this was long before the word of the FIFA disciplinary committee was law) by the Brazilian authorities led to a reprieve and he took his place in the starting line-up. Though Garrincha was less effective against Czechoslovakia, Brazil were still able to emerge victorious.

This was the pinnacle of Garrincha's career: his persistent drinking and womanising got the better of him, and he died in 1983 leaving a legacy that included a trail of illegitimate children, wife-beating and drink-driving offences. A genius with a football at his feet, Garrincha's human failings led him down a path that has become all too familiar for a succession of maverick footballers.

Ignition key: wine, women and song (or any two of the three).

GEORGE BEST

(Northern Ireland, Forward-Winger)

'The Fifth Beatle', in many ways, George Best epitomised the Swinging Sixties. He was a long-haired cavalier, extravagantly gifted, a free spirit and a shameless exponent of free love, parading around Manchester nightspots (one of which he owned) a string of attractive girlfriends – alleged to include Germaine Greer, Barbara Windsor, Susan George and Lynsey de Paul.

His football was as carefree as his lifestyle. Fast and skilful, but strong as well so tough to dispossess, Best was the complete forward. Like a later Man United star, Cristiano Ronaldo, he was good in the air for a winger. Best came up against some of the game's 'celebrated' hard men – Tommy Smith, 'Chopper' Harris, Norman Hunter – and he would delight in taunting them, no matter what retribution they exacted on his shins.

United's front three of Best, Charlton and Law was as good a trio as any English club has fielded, and, on form, they were the best in Europe – proving it in 1968 when Best destroyed Benfica in injury time in the European final.

The club's subsequent decline was matched by the player's – only a brief flicker at Fulham in the mid-seventies interrupted the flow of reports of lack of fitness and missing training and drinking.

Best's problems with booze were his eventual undoing. A couple of convictions for drunk driving and more than one public appearance in a parlous state did nothing to spoil his popularity, but the drink affected his health. Best survived one liver transplant but couldn't kick the habit and died before he reached sixty.

Ignition key: will auto-combust if doused with alcohol.

PAUL GASCOIGNE

(England, Attacking Midfielder)

Too ready to play the gurning buffoon? Too fond of the drink? Too prone to crass and inappropriate gestures?

Paul Gascoigne was without question the most talented British footballer since George Best. He had a low centre of gravity, tree-trunk legs and was almost impossible to knock off the ball. Allied to terrific close control, a good range of passing, deceptive change of pace and competent finishing, he was a challenge for any opponent when on his game. It is no coincidence that England's best performances in major tournaments since 1966 came at the 1990 World Cup and 1996 European Championship, when Gascoigne was the pivotal influence on the side. His inventiveness and element of unpredictability kept opponents on the back foot.

Unfortunately, with the unpredictable nature came errors of judgement: some tomfoolery, drinking, weight issues and bad luck with injuries led to his career stalling at crucial times.

Under the relaxed management of Terry Venables, Gascoigne thrived at Tottenham in the early 1990s and for England in 1996. He put in some outstanding performances for Rangers under Graeme Souness, and seemed to have resurrected his international career, only to be left out of the 1998 World Cup squad by Glenn Hoddle. Oddly for such a creative player, Hoddle the manager mistrusted Gascoigne's maverick talent.

More understandable was Gascoigne's failure to make the most of his time at Lazio. It was asking a lot of Gascoigne, away from his mates and his mentor, to adapt to a foreign culture. Like many before him, and doubtless many to come, Gascoigne was consumed by the intensity of the heat from the media spotlight. Ten years later and he might have found himself with an entourage capable of guiding him through that particular minefield, but too often Gazza made a misguided choice and paid the price. Now a peripheral figure, Gascoigne really was a marvellous player.

Ignition key: if mixed with alcohol will combust but if mixed with Germans will produce salt water.

ERIC CANTONA

(France, Forward)

L'enfant terrible of French (and Premier League) football, Eric Cantona was a wonderfully talented and entertainingly cryptic player with his inbuilt powder keg of intolerance and pent-up frustration.

Before he came to England, bought by Howard Wilkinson to add spark to Leeds's (ultimately successful) title challenge, Cantona had been employed by four clubs in the previous three years, and had numerous *contretemps* on his record.

In 1987 he punched a teammate in the face at Auxerre and was later banned for two months for a reckless tackle. At Marseilles he kicked the ball into the crowd and got a twelve-month international ban for referring to the national coach as a 'bag of shit'. Cantona's international career never reflected his talent – he was slightly too early for the great generation of players who won the World Cup in 1998.

A hat-trick in the Charity Shield at the start of the 1992–3 season prompted Alex Ferguson to make an inquiry and, by November, Cantona was a Manchester

United player. Finally he had a manager who was equipped to deal with his temperament and fully utilise his talent. The trophies came freely, and Ferguson rode out the red cards and tantrums with aplomb. Even the notorious kung-fu kick, when Cantona launched himself into the crowd to attack an abusive fan, didn't earn him the sack. United waited patiently for Cantona to serve an eight-month suspension and waited another three months for him to return to form. When he did, they overturned a ten-point deficit as Kevin Keegan's hapless Newcastle team imploded at the end of the season. Cantona finished the season as the first overseas captain to hold up the FA Cup as United won the double.

A year later, in 1997, he was gone, retired at thirty years old, leaving the game for a media career in the same enigmatic fashion in which he had served it. A couple of film appearances and some typically inflammatory outbursts have kept up his profile and he remains a colourful and controversial sideshow.

Ignition key: if mixed with perceived slights or ignorance will explode, often violently.

ROY KEANE

(Ireland, Midfielder)

Everything Keane has done he did with full commitment and stood by his decision and his actions, however crass they may appear.

The reckless and dangerous tackle on Alf-Inge Haaland was a crude end to an ongoing feud between the two players. The verbal assault on his manager at the 2002 World Cup was unpardonable. Not even his friends in the squad felt able to defend the outburst and Keane's lack of contrition was based more on stubbornness. The fact that his complaints about team training conditions were justified was a trigger, but not a valid reason.

Keane earned eleven red cards during his career, although he did make some effort to curb his temper in his later years. Not that the players under his management at Sunderland or Ipswich would have believed it. The response wasn't always as desired and his managerial career has been hitherto uninspired.

As a player, Keane's drive and combative energy were allied to no little skill and he proved a perfect replacement for the ageing Bryan Robson at Manchester United. Perhaps his finest moment was the 1999 Champions League semi-final against Juventus. The first leg finished 1-1 and United were 2-0 down in Turin after only eleven minutes. Keane drove his teammates forward by force of will and hauled them back into the game by half-time. A late Andy Cole winner sealed a remarkable turnaround. Keane rightly took the plaudits for producing a stunning display, even after receiving a yellow card that he knew meant missing the final. It was the mark of the man: no retreat, no surrender. It isn't always the right way.

Ignition key: mix views contrary to those held by Keane – stand back and watch the fireworks.

ZINEDINE ZIDANE

(France, Attacking Midfielder)

Zinedine Zidane is known as 'Zizou' in France, an affectionate name to celebrate one of the country's best-loved footballers, perhaps the second greatest in their history.

Zidane didn't have an explosive beginning to his career, earning his dues at Cannes and Bordeaux before the big-money teams came looking. He was twenty-two before he made his debut for the international team and it took him another two or three years to establish himself as a regular – a poor showing at the 1996 European Championship led people to suggest he was overrated.

Two years later at the World Cup on home soil, Zidane and his French colleagues put that right. Despite lacking a striker of international quality, let alone world-class, France battled their way through to the final. An obdurate defence helped and the absence of a quality striker was compensated in part by the quality of the midfield players, Zidane primary among them.

Two thumping headers against Brazil in the final won the day as Ronaldo's mystery illness led to a limp and uninspired performance from the favourites.

Now Zidane was a national hero and he fully lived up to his billing at the European Championship in 2000 as France cemented a notable double. Some scintillating performances for Real Madrid over the next couple of years confirmed Zidane's standing as one of the top players in the world. A fantastic volley to win the Champions League final against Bayer Leverkusen in 2002 remains one of the best goals scored in a major final – the marking was a bit lightweight but as a display of perfect balance and technique it takes some beating.

Zidane came out of international retirement to help France qualify for the 2006 World Cup Finals and played a starring role as a side full of veterans exceeded expectations by making it all the way to the final. A fitting finale was set up and he scored the opening goal from the penalty spot.

What came after was an anti-climax: Zidane failed to see out the match after being sent off for headbutting Italy's Marco Materazzi. All kind of stories were banded around about why Zidane reacted so violently. They are all irrelevant: he was an experienced professional in a crucial match. Fourteen red cards in a career suggest a dark side – it is an ugly statistic.

Ignition key: seemingly random acts can cause this element to self-destruct.

Corrosives

Some elements are harmful. They may have good qualities too, but their general effect on the game is negative and damaging. This may be for a specific action they have taken or because they have left a damaging legacy.

This is a subjective group, by its very nature. Others may have a much more positive view of one or more of these individuals but, however successful Paolo Rossi was, he will always be remembered as the man who came back after a ban for taking bribes; however important Herrera's influence as a coach, he took some of the game's innocence with him; and whatever good Sepp Blatter did for football in the Third World, few believe it was done in a spirit of altruism. Leave these elements well alone – they may poison your favourite game.

Column 18

78 9 **Si** Sindelar	85 – **Bt** Blatter
79 7 **Ga** Garrincha	86 – **Hv** Havelange
80 7 **Be** Best	87 – **He** Herrera
81 19 **Gz** Gascoigne	88 5/10 **Rt** Rattín
82 7 **Ca** Cantona	89 20 **Ro** Rossi
83 16 **Ke** Keane	90 10 **Ln** Lentini
84 10 **Zd** Zidane	91 – **Mu** Murdoch
	92 7/9 **Su** Suárez

85   –

Bt

Blatter

SEPP BLATTER

(Switzerland, Administrator)

Pending investigations in Switzerland and the United States, forbid the polemic that would otherwise sit here. Suffice to say that the biggest crisis football's major body has faced or will probably ever face has come during Blatter's tenure as President of FIFA. That is damnation enough. If you are at the tip of the umbrella, you can't avoid the rain.

Blatter did SOME good work extending FIFA's hand more extensively to the poorer, less historically influential parts of the footballing world, but the mess of corruption will taint this legacy. A few words from Blatter and one admirer:

On John Terry conducting an affair with his teammate's wife: 'If this had happened in, let's say, Latin countries then I think he would have been applauded.'
Sepp Blatter

Downplaying the altercation between Luis Suárez and Patrice Evra: 'There is no racism, there is maybe one of the players towards the other, he has a word or a gesture which is not the correct one, but also the one who is affected by that, he should say it's a game, we are in a game.' *Sepp Blatter*

'The work FIFA do is noble. Unlike many other associations that proclaim nice, well intentioned goals, they work to realise them. This has no precedent in humanitarian spheres.' *Vladimir Putin*

86   –

Hv

Havelange

JOÃO HAVELANGE

(Brazil, Administrator)

Just in case you thought corruption in FIFA is a new thing, I thought I'd remind you about this FIFA President. Havelange, a Brazilian former Olympic swimmer (of no great pedigree), became a member of the International

Olympic Committee (IOC) in 1963. In 1974 he also wrestled the Presidency of FIFA off Stanley Rous. He held the latter office until 1998 and remained an IOC member until 2011.

In his time as FIFA President, Havelange worked to reduce the authority of the European footballing superpowers and increase the game's profile in the developing world. Did he do this out of a sense of altruism? Was any money he made along the way merely incidental?

Havelange has resigned all his commissions (allegedly due to ill health) and has been stripped of his lifetime position of Honorary President of FIFA.

A number of journalists, Andrew Jennings foremost among them, brought evidence to light that Havelange and his associates had taken millions in gifts during their FIFA tenure. The findings were damaging enough to force the resignations of Havelange and Ricardo Teixeira, his former son-in-law and head of the Brazilian Football Confederation.

Many believe that the misdeeds made public are merely the tip of the iceberg.

HELENIO HERRERA

(Argentina, Coach)

Catenaccio, they called it. The Swiss team under Karl Rappan in the 1930s used a flexible version of the conventional WM formation that became known as 'the bolt' (*verrou* in French) for the extra defensive capabilities it gave the team. Rappan developed the system to compensate for a perceived lack of quality individuals in his team, placing the emphasis more on teamwork than individual brilliance. The essence of the system was a three-man defence including a deep-lying sweeper, with two attacking full backs, three midfield players and two forwards.

At the end of the 1950s, Helenio Herrera moved from Barcelona to a new job at Inter Milan. Herrera used his knowledge of the history of the game and his experience to devise a system that allowed Inter to soak up pressure but also to be able to counter-attack at speed and bring their own creative players into play. He also instigated a brutal training regime and restrictions on players' freedoms that were unusual at the time.

Herrera's sides were uncompromising, and had a win-at-all-costs attitude. Both Rangers and Liverpool complained bitterly about Inter's tactics and their coercion of the officials as both were beaten in Milan while Inter made their way to winning the European Cup in 1965. Inter racked up trophies but made few friends.

Herrera set out a blueprint for negative and stifling football – 'parking the bus' is a modern paraphrase for the same approach. It is a legitimate tactic, but no one would ever claim it is a good thing.

ANTONIO RATTÍN

(Argentina, Defensive Midfielder)

What is the so-called 'spirit of the game'? It's a commitment to try to win a game by acceptable means, and that doesn't just mean by not breaking the rules, but also by showing respect for fans, officials and the opposition.

It became trendy in later years to make apologies for Antonio Rattín and suggest that 'homer' refereeing and provocation were the principal reasons for his sending off at the 1966 World Cup. Critics point to the aggressive tackling of Jack Charlton, Nobby Stiles and Alan Ball as an indication that England, not Argentina, were the sinners here.

England were a physical side in 1966, but then most sides in 1966 were physical. Brazil were practically disqualified from the tournament, while the West Germany–USSR semi-final was arguably twice as rough as the England–Argentina game. Both Argentina and England were wary of the other team's ability, and both resorted to spoiling tactics rather than creative skills.

Rattín started the game in paranoid mood; he lunged recklessly at Bobby Charlton and was booked. He questioned every decision made against his team and was then pulled up for another heavy tackle on Hurst. Rattín's ensuing verbal tirade aimed at the German referee was what, ultimately, got him sent off. Rattín refused to leave the field, instead demanding a translator.

Alf Ramsey called the Argentina team animals after the game. Ramsey's comments were inflammatory but that doesn't excuse Rattín's behaviour.

Rattín spat on the spirit of the game as well as at a ball-boy as he was escorted off the field.

PAOLO ROSSI

89   20

Ro

Rossi

(Italy, Forward)

Italian football has been beset by financial scandals. Many of them involve the dodgy dealings of a president or officials – Italian clubs created the model for the autocratic hire-'em-and-fire-'em owner so prevalent today. A few have involved very high-profile players and clubs.

In 2015, there was a new wave of arrests and prosecutions for fixing lower division matches: the less high profile a game, the easier it is for a syndicate to manipulate the outcome.

There have been similar issues in Germany and England but in Italy there had been arrests and prosecutions in 2011–12, including former internationals Cristiano Doni and Giuseppe Signori; in 2006, which ended with Juventus being relegated and point deductions for Milan, Lazio, Fiorentina and Reggina; in 1986, with Udinese, Lazio and Cagliari being the high-profile clubs involved; and in 1980, with Milan and Lazio (again!) as the principal culprits.

One of the players prosecuted and banned in the 1980 scandal was Paolo Rossi, an Italian international striker on loan at Perugia. Rossi has always maintained his innocence but has never been officially reprieved. His ban, originally of three years, was reduced to two and he reappeared for Juventus at the end of the 1981–2 season.

Conveniently, he was playing again just in time to make the Italy squad for the 1982 World Cup Finals tournament (and Italy were desperately short of a finisher). Rossi played poorly in the early rounds but coach Enzo Bearzot stuck with him and was rewarded with a scintillating hat-trick in a classic match against Brazil, two more goals in the semi-final and the first in a 3-1 win over West Germany in the final.

It may seem harsh to pick on Rossi but no other player implicated in overt corruption has achieved such conspicuous success after coming back from a ban.

GIANLUIGI LENTINI

(Italy, Winger/Forward)

Inflated transfer fees are a poison that has ruined many clubs and distorted many assessments of a player's value. At time of writing, the world's most expensive footballer is Gareth Bale; before that it was Cristiano Ronaldo, before that Kaká, Zidane, Figo, Crespo… all terrific players. In 1992 it was Gianluigi Lentini.

Lentini was a really promising player. Some terrific performances for Torino earned him a £13 million move to Milan in 1992, a few months after Gianluca Vialli's £12.5 million move from Sampdoria to Juventus, making him the world's most expensive player. Lentini was a skilful, balanced winger with a decent delivery, but he wasn't yet an established international and it was a gamble at best.

It's hard to say whether Lentini would have justified his fee, as his career was derailed by a bad motor accident; he came back to football but was never as potent. Unlucky, yes he was, but he is also a symbol of the madness of investment in footballers.

This madness isn't unique to Italy. In 1979, Manchester City paid nearly £1.5 million for Steve Daley, a journeyman midfield player. Real Betis paid over £20 million for Denilson – that works out at around £1.5 million per goal he scored in seven years. Manchester United paid £28 million for Juan Sebastián Verón, a really top-class player, but he never adapted to English football.

The problem with one side paying above the odds for a lesser player is that it inflates the market for others and the whole market escalates. It all helps fuel the current state of play where the rich get richer from all the TV pickings and collaborate to push prices beyond the less fortunate or successful clubs. This is one financial model that can't be blamed on the USA – their draft system gives all the teams a more level playing field and it isn't just the same old names at the business end of the season every year.

RUPERT MURDOCH

(Australia and United States, Media Magnate)

If you want to watch live football on TV, you have to pay for the privilege and sign up to Sky or BT Sport or one of the many subscription channels. Same if you want to watch the Ryder Cup, test cricket or a high-profile boxing match. The hype is hysterical and unconsidered; the subscription channels expect viewers to believe that Nobody United against Nondescript City will be a pulsating classic when everyone knows it will be a dour affair between two average teams transmitted on a Monday night so Sky can fulfil their obligations to the lesser lights as well as showing Chelsea v. Man United. And Murdoch is responsible. News Corp. saw, astutely, that pay-per-view sport was a unique selling point, and along with their movie packages the sports channels became their flagship enterprise. As movies became a less defensible currency so the sport became more and more important and Sky invested more and more money into the product and advertising.

The money the fans pay to Sky (and competitors like BT Sport) isn't always directed to the parts of the game that need development and funding, like small clubs and grass-roots football. The inequality between the haves and the have-nots has deepened both in the UK and across Europe, and the amount of money going into the pockets of less than exceptional players and their agents is, frankly, obscene.

The money has leeched the soul from the game and made it the playground of egotistical billionaires and officials and lawyers and marketing men.

LUIS SUÁREZ

(Uruguay, Forward)

There have been more than a few players over the years whose unbecoming conduct has had the decency brigade foaming at the mouth. Paolo Di Canio, Ben Thatcher and Joey Barton all received lengthy bans for indiscretion or violence. The game has always been prone to the odd red-mist episode: Kevin Keegan and Billy Bremner in the Charity Shield, Cantona's kung-fu kick and Zidane's headbutt are unforgettable parts of football history. But biting people? Come on. The episode at the 2014 World Cup was on top of two previous convictions for the same offence and a ban for making a racist remark to Patrice Evra.

Almost as disappointing as the bite Suárez took out of Italian defender Giorgio Chellini was the reaction: one of feigned innocence and a misplaced sense of persecution. The Uruguay management team closed ranks, just furthering Suárez's delusion that he was wronged.

Suárez is a fantastic footballer. Judged on ability alone he is on the same level as Messi or Cristiano Ronaldo and has a better team ethic than either. He lacks the extreme pace of those two notable contemporaries, but his movement is superb, his touch instinctive and his finishing precise, occasionally spectacular. He left Liverpool for Barcelona post-incident and while Liverpool lapsed back into mediocrity, Barcelona regained their splendour and won the Champions League and Spanish title. Barcelona should be grateful but Suárez is lucky to be playing. If his profile and ability were less he would never play again, but he is a marketable asset (see Murdoch entry above) and so will be protected.

Rare Earth Metals

The next two sections are the loose cannons in the table, the entries that don't conform to the patterns outlined in the previous sections. They sit between Columns 13 and 14 but stand alone in their glorious quirkiness.

Polymorphs

Polymorphs

Some football personalities leave a legacy that goes beyond their abilities as a player or coach. It may be an attitude or approach to the sport that is different in spirit to that of their contemporaries, or it may be a talent or gift that allows them to flourish beyond the confines of the game. Whatever the reason, this is a group who are not defined solely by their ability to play football.

93   –
Ak
Alcock

CHARLES ALCOCK

(England, Administrator)

Alcock was a member of the FA Committee from 1866 and became the organisation's fourth secretary in 1870. In addition to inaugurating international fixtures between England and Scotland, he also put forward a proposal for a competitive competition called the FA Cup, an idea that came to fruition in 1872.

The first competition saw Wanderers (no relation to either Bolton or Wolverhampton) defeat the Royal Engineers 1-0 in the final, with Alcock captaining the winning side. There was nothing sinister in this: most of the game's early administrators were also keen players. Alcock also played for England and scored against the Scots in a 2-2 draw in 1875.

In 1877 the two slightly differing sets of rules as laid down in London and Sheffield were standardised under Alcock's watch into the first definitive Laws of the Game. The man who drew up the initial London rules, Ebenezer Cobb Morley, was the FA's first Secretary and another prime mover in the birth of competitive football.

Very much a sporting polymath, Alcock was a keen cricketer and committee man at Surrey. The first FA Cup final was played at Surrey's Oval ground in Kennington, London, and in 1880 Alcock arranged the first game of test match cricket between England and Australia at the same venue.

DENIS COMPTON

(England, Winger, Cricketer)

It is impossible to imagine combining a top-class cricket career with a professional football career now, such is the overlap between seasons. But there was a time after the Second World War when it was relatively common.

The most recent dual internationals were Arthur Milton and Willie Watson, who both played their last test match in 1959. Watson was the more successful; he played four times for England at football (and was an unused squad member at the 1950 World Cup Finals) and twenty-three times in a stop-start test career.

Much earlier, the legendary polymath C. B. Fry played at both games for England, won an FA Cup winner's medal with Southampton, missed out on a rugby union blue at Oxford through injury and held the world long-jump record for a while. Those were the days. It is alleged (and he claimed it to be true) that he was offered the throne of Albania!

Perhaps the most notable dual career was that of Denis Compton. Compton was a cricketer of the highest quality, a dashing cavalier batsman who scored runs even against the all-conquering 1948 Australian side. Compton amassed nearly 6,000 test runs despite losing time to the Second World War and he averaged over fifty – a rare statistic in the 1950s. As a footballer he was a nippy, skilful winger who won a league title and an FA Cup winner's medal for Arsenal just after the war. It is suggested he would have played for England had his cricketing duties not limited his availability. His brother Leslie won one cap for England aged thirty-eight and remains the oldest outfield debutant. He also shared in his brother's cricketing successes at Middlesex, but never made the test team.

Compton was, like many cricketers of his day, a little bit eccentric. He once turned up for a test match without his kit. It is alleged he used an old bat from the trophy room and proceeded to score a hundred.

SÓCRATES

(Brazil, Playmaker/Political Activist)

Sócrates made his debut for Brazil when he was twenty-five; before that he stayed an amateur with Botafogo-SP (not the famous Botafogo but a lower division side) while he completed his medical studies. He moved to the Corinthians club and was picked for Brazil sixty times; he captained the talented and entertaining side that lost to Italy at the 1982 World Cup.

Sócrates was a tall, long-striding player with a big beard and a headband, aping the look of his hero Che Guevara (he cited Fidel Castro and John Lennon as other major influences). He had a casual air and seemed to stroll through a match, but the long legs could shift when a goalscoring opportunity presented itself. His attacking midfield partnership with Falcão and Zico produced cavalier football reminiscent of the glory days of 1970 – and if you've got this far through the book, you know that's some compliment.

In 2004, in one of football's more bizarre signings, Sócrates agreed to play for non-league club Garforth Town for a month, aged fifty. He managed twelve minutes. There were signs that his heavy smoking and love of a drink were taking their toll.

Sócrates was an integral part of the Corinthians Democracy movement in the 1980s, when the club gave power back to the fans and the locals as a gesture of defiance aimed at the military government.

He remained a prominent spokesperson for the unrepresented until his sad death from a stomach infection in 2011. On the same day his beloved Corinthians clinched-the league title and 50,000 fans gave the Che Guevara clenched-fist salute with which Sócrates used to celebrate his goals.

GEORGE WEAH

(Liberia, Forward/Politician)

George Weah had a nomadic career, playing in Liberia, Cameroon, France, Italy, England and the United Arab Emirates. When he first moved to France in 1988 to play for AS Monaco under Arsène Wenger there weren't too many African stars playing in Europe. Even fewer managed to carve out the sort of career Weah enjoyed. He won league titles in France and Italy with PSG and Milan and added an FA Cup winner's medal in a loan spell at Chelsea towards the end of his career.

In 1995 Weah was voted FIFA World Player of the Year, the first and so far only African player to win the award. He was a fast, athletic forward with decent technique and bags of power. He liked to run at the defence Brazilian style, but he was smart and could hold up play well when required.

Weah never lost touch with his roots. Like many African players he ensured a lot of the money he earned went back to help people in his homeland. Liberia was a riven country – a first civil war saw the military dictator Samuel Doe ousted and executed, only to be replaced by another dictator, Charles Taylor. A second war saw Taylor deposed and arrested (he was sentenced to fifty years in prison at The Hague), and a democratic election was called.

Weah formed a new party, the Congress for Democratic Change, and ran for president against a former Taylor supporter, Ellen Johnson Sirleaf, in 2005. He was defeated, but returned in 2014 to win a Senate seat in opposition to Sirleaf's son.

VINNIE JONES

(England, Defensive Midfielder/Actor)

Vinnie's football career shouldn't take up too much of our time. His fearsome image was a key part of the armoury of a steely and intimidating Wimbledon team, who won their only major trophy in 1988, the FA Cup. Nine caps for Wales (he had a Welsh grandparent) are a fair summary of Jones's level.

It is the astute use of his hard-man image that picks Jones out from the crowd. A confident and amusing debut in Guy Ritchie's 1998 Brit gangster film *Lock, Stock and Two Smoking Barrels* set up two decades of regular work as a character actor and go-to tough guy. One of Jones's assets as a footballer included knowing his limitations and playing within them; he brought the same self-awareness to his acting, showing a canny knack for choosing roles to play to his strengths that didn't overexpose him.

Footballers tend to make poor actors – watch *Escape to Victory* if you don't believe me – and Jones deserves enormous credit for bucking that trend, carving out a second career of some longevity that no one would have expected.

RENÉ HIGUITA

(Colombia, Goalkeeper)

El Loco, they called him, which translates as 'madman' or 'nutter'. In 1988, Higuita came out of his goal to meet a through ball and instead of hoofing it into the stands he took it neatly around Gary Lineker and slipped it to the full back. This was not a piece of showboating (though Higuita wasn't afraid of a bit of amateur dramatics), but part of Colombia's high pressing game – having a goalkeeper acting as sweeper gave them liberty to hold their defensive line further up the field (like Neuer and Germany in 2014). The game, which finished in a 1-1 draw, was seen as a breakthrough result for Colombia in Europe.

Higuita's attempts to play sweeper weren't always successful. At the 1990 World Cup, Colombia were in extra time against a powerful Cameroon side with the old fox, Roger Milla, on as a substitute. Milla scored the first goal of the game and three minutes later Higuita tried to round him on the edge of the box. Milla read the feint and dispossessed the goalkeeper – Colombia lost 2-1.

In the 1994 World Cup, Colombia defeated Argentina 5-0 to qualify (in Buenos Aires) and had the most talented side in their history. Except for Higuita, their goalkeeper and talisman, who was only just out of jail for acting as the go-between in a kidnapping case arranged by the Colombian drug cartels. Colombia flopped in the tournament and the luckless Andrés Escobar, who scored an own goal against the US, was made the scapegoat.

Then in the 1995 *Copa América*, Higuita dribbled out of his area after saving a free kick and provoked a punch-up by executing a flamboyant dive after a thumping tackle. In the same year, Higuita famously produced his trademark 'scorpion kick' against England in another friendly at Wembley. This trick involved waiting for a long-distance shot or cross that wash looping rather than ferocious in nature, and instead of catching the ball or clearing it conventionally, performing a forward flip and clearing the ball with the inverted heels – in this case beyond the penalty area. Words don't do it justice – get on YouTube and see the hilarity/genius/madness of this genuine entertainer for yourself.

JOSÉ LUIS CHILAVERT

(Paraguay, Goalkeeper)

If footballing prowess is judged by size of ego, this player would be a world beater. A larger than life South American motor mouth, Chilavert has opinions on himself (generally positive), opponents (not always complimentary), press (borderline abusive) and politicians (downright contemptuous). He is not always out of line – his dislike of inequality in South America and his self-deprecating humour are endearing – but some of his vitriol could be offensive.

He made too many errors to be regarded as a great goalkeeper but what sets him apart is his goalscoring record. Eight goals in seventy-one internationals is an unremarkable statistic – except for a goalkeeper. Adept at thumping away penalties, Chilavert extended this dead-ball expertise to charging forward to have a pop at goal from free kicks. His hit rate wasn't bad; it wasn't just a show-pony trick (although that element was never far away). He once scored a hat-trick in a league match and was only denied by a fine Iker Casillas save from becoming the first keeper to score in a World Cup Finals tournament. Chilavert was a rare success story from a poor South American background. A boy who never wore shoes until he was seven who became an international star.

DAVID BECKHAM

(England, Wide Midfielder/Professional Celebrity)

There's nothing to say here about David Beckham that you probably don't already know. That's why he is here. No other player has made his presence at big events, both in his own country and overseas, so ubiquitous. The sight of 'Becks' and his wife grinning out of the pages of society magazines, tabloids and Sunday supplements is as much part of twenty-first-century living as Facebook and banking scandals.

Beckham was the first footballer who became a global brand. His talent and looks became such a desirable entity that clubs bought him as an asset not just a footballer. He wasn't in the same class as a player as Zidane and Figo but he lined up alongside them at Real Madrid because Real wanted recognisable faces as well as good players.

His value to LA Galaxy and Major League Soccer wasn't so much as a player, but more as a brand to raise recognition of soccer in the US and recognition of US soccer elsewhere in the world. It worked.

Beckham was a damn fine footballer who worked hard for every team he played for. It was sheer hard work and practice that made Beckham possibly the finest striker of a dead ball, certainly in the English game, that football has ever seen.

The goal he scored early in his career against Wimbledon when he lobbed Neil Sullivan from the halfway line was sublime, and his performance against Greece in a crucial World Cup qualifier (when he carried England while everyone else played badly): that was raw patriotic passion of the best kind.

One other thing: he has done it all with a smile. No sour words, no resentment, lots of stick from the tabloids, which he has borne with grace, and genuine care for his family and friends.

Trace
Elements

There are hundreds of these, elements who flicker and illuminate, but whose role in the football universe is, in hindsight, a minor one. They are meteors and comets, not planets, but they had their moment(s).

LEN SHACKLETON

(England, Forward)

Distrusted by the authorities and the England selectors, Len Shackleton was the forerunner of the so-called maverick players of the sixties and seventies: George Best, Rodney Marsh, Stan Bowles, Frank Worthington, Duncan McKenzie and all those flair in flares guys.

Once when through on goal he stopped and pretended to look at his watch before advancing on goal. He would often stop the ball on the goal line and wait for a defender to come and challenge him before poking it into the net. Many opposition players took exception and found it disrespectful, so Shackleton had to be tough to take the kickings he was often handed by lesser talents.

It wasn't that Shackleton was unfit or that he was rebellious or had a flaky lifestyle, he just wanted to play the game in a fun way, not stick to regimented tactics or hold a defensive line.

Shackleton started at Bradford Park Avenue but didn't play much league football until after the Second World War when he was twenty-four. He earned a move to Newcastle but didn't fit in and he moved south to Sunderland – not a move likely to endear him to the Toon. He was a great hit there and the fans loved him, but some critics suggest that his presence in the side wasn't always positive: they point to the fact that the club won nothing despite spending more money on players than any of their rivals.

On his retirement Shackleton published his autobiography, *The Clown Prince of Soccer.* It featured a chapter called 'The Average Director's Knowledge of Football'. The next page was blank.

EDUARD STRELTSOV

(Russia, Attacking Midfielder)

The best player you've never heard of, that's who. Streltsov was a massively talented inside forward with Torpedo Moscow in the 1950s. He won twenty-one caps for the Soviet Union between 1955 and 1958 and another seventeen between 1966 and 1968. Streltsov was quick, skilful, strong and aggressive, with good technique and a particular gift for using back-heeled passes to release colleagues into space. He was brilliant in the Soviets' campaign at the 1956 Olympic Games, but missed the final after the coach (bizarrely) concluded that he was only effective if his teammate Valentin Ivanov was playing, and Ivanov was injured. The Soviets were approaching the 1958 World Cup as genuine contenders.

What happened between 1958 and 1966? Streltsov and two colleagues were arrested, tried and sentenced for rape. Streltsov enjoyed a lifestyle at odds with the Soviet notion of a good citizen. He was mistrusted by the apparatchiks and there are rumours that he may well have been set up. He equally may well have been guilty; such is the obfuscation surrounding what took place in the Soviet Union at the height of the Cold War that we will never know for sure.

Streltsov was freed in 1963 and soon acquired a cult following while playing for his works team. When Brezhnev replaced Khrushchev he was persuaded to lift the lifetime ban on Streltsov playing at the top level and he returned to play for Torpedo Moscow and win those last few caps for his country. He wasn't as quick or strong – the Gulag had taken its toll – but the football brain was still there and he played in a deeper playmaking role, finally winning a league title in 1965.

103   9

Al

Albert

FLÓRIÁN ALBERT

(Hungary, Forward)

Did you think Hungary were finished as a national team when the great team of the 1950s broke up? In fact, Hungary qualified for both World Cup tournaments in the 1960s and also reached the semi-finals of the 1964 European Nations' Cup (As the European Championship was originally called). They rebuilt the team from scratch after the mass exodus following the 1956 Soviet invasion and by 1962 just goalkeeper Gyula Grosics remained from the glory days, but some good young players had come through.

The defender Kálmán Mészöly was a cultured ball-playing central defender who liked banging away penalties. Lajos Tichy was a compact and busy goalscoring forward, and in the squad was a rapid winger called János Farkas. By 1966 they had added Ferenc Bene, a potent goalscorer with Újpesti Dózsa.

First among equals was Flórián Albert, socks around ankles, dictating play from the deep-lying centre-forward position pioneered by Nándor Hidegkuti. He could look disinterested at times and tended to disappear if closely and well marked, but if he was in the mood the opposition were in trouble. His close control was exceptional, his vision and passing first rate and his shooting dangerous, usually opting for low rasping drives to make the goalkeeper work.

Albert's best day for Hungary came against Brazil in the 1966 World Cup. It looked like the absent Pelé had decided to turn out for the other team and Hungary ran out easy winners (Brazil – always talented but not so good with the man-marking). A slide-rule pass for Tichy to latch on to and cross so Farkas could belt home on the volley was the highlight. Albert's best day for Ferencváros, his only club, was winning the Inter Cities Cup (later UEFA Cup), the only time a Hungarian team won a European club trophy.

ALAN HUDSON

(England, Midfielder)

Alan Hudson was a fantastic player. He started with Chelsea in the glamour years, joining Peter Osgood and Charlie Cooke in an entertaining side that finished third in the league in 1970 and won the FA Cup – Hudson, still only eighteen, missed the final through injury. The youngster was a prompter and a creator, never a great goalscorer, but he brought the best out of lesser players around him with his craft and vision.

As Chelsea hit money trouble, Hudson was sold to Stoke City and became the fulcrum of the club's most successful spell. Stoke finished fifth for two successive seasons and Hudson earned a long overdue call-up to the England side in 1975.

In the first game the opponents were reigning world and European champions West Germany. England used Hudson alongside Alan Ball and Colin Bell in midfield and the energy and tackling of those two allowed Hudson to show his full range of playmaking skills, with England running out 2-0 winners. When they won the next match 5-0 against Cyprus, with Malcolm Macdonald scoring all five, a bright new dawn was heralded. Unfortunately, Hudson was injured for the next game and Don Revie, ever mistrustful of what he deemed maverick talents, didn't use him again.

Hudson was again sold to ease a club's debt, this time to Arsenal. He never got on at Highbury and by twenty-seven he was playing in the circus that was the US league. It was a loss. He was a drinker and sometimes a contrary character, but that was hardly novel in the seventies. He was also a fantastic footballer.

Hudson was hit by a car in 1997 and has needed crutches since; he has alleged the incident was a deliberate attempt on his life.

TEÓFILO CUBILLAS

(Peru, Attacking Midfielder)

Peru were a bit of a surprise package at a couple of World Cup tournaments way back when, and they won the *Copa América* in 1975. One of the principal reasons was the presence of a genuine world-class player in Teófilo Cubillas, an attacking midfield player with a vicious shot.

Peru turned up in Mexico in 1970 having qualified (at Argentina's expense) for the first time in forty years and never having won a game at the World Cup Finals. That record looked secure as they went 2-0 down against Bulgaria, but then Cubillas inspired a great comeback. It took Brazil to stop the adventure, but *El Nene* (the kid) scored in every game.

Cubillas was just as influential as Peru beat Brazil and Colombia to win the *Copa América*, and three years later he was back at the World Cup in a group with the Dutch and Scotland. The Scottish manager was Ally MacLeod, and he didn't do his homework. He fielded two slow full backs against a team with one of the great passers of the ball and two express wingers, Juan Muñante and Juan Carlos Oblitas. Cubillas scored twice, the second a brilliant free kick curled around the wall with the outside of his foot. Peru reached the second stage but were beaten by strong sides in Poland, Brazil and Argentina. By the time the 1982 Finals came around even Cubillas, now thirty-three, couldn't coax a weak side into the latter stages.

It was Peru's best spell in their history, orchestrated by their best ever player – one of the most ferocious strikers the game has known.

Cubillas played for Alianza Lima in Peru, had spells in Switzerland and Portugal but also enjoyed a four-year spell with Fort Lauderdale Strikers in the NASL; he was one of the few to take the whole thing seriously and was a great favourite in Florida.

GUDNI BERGSSON

(Iceland, Defender)

Forgive the author, for I am indulging myself here.

Gudni Bergsson was a giant for Bolton Wanderers and was one of the most underrated defenders to play in the Premier League. When he was released by Tottenham approaching thirty years old in 1995, Bergsson must have thought he was nearly done – so much so that he started his studies to become a lawyer. A bit prematurely as it turned out, as 'The Iceman' managed another eight years as the first name on the Wanderers team sheet.

Bergsson and Bolton had their ups and downs: the team struggled to hold on to Premier League status at first, and Bergsson was one of the few who could hold his own at that level. He settled at centre half (he was mainly used at right back at Tottenham) and was an uncompromising presence – rarely falling foul of the referees he had the Italian knack of fouling discreetly.

As Bolton toughened up under Sam Allardyce, Bergsson was persuaded to keep going for another year or two to help them cement their place at the top table. They did, and it was no small thanks to Iceland's best ever defender (they also had their best ever striker for a while, but Eidur Gudjohnsen will keep for another book).

Bergsson's debut for Wanderers was in the 1995 League Cup final when he came on as a substitute to try and get a grip on a rampant Steve McManaman. Bergsson's first touch was a cross for Bolton's goal, which brought it back to 2-1. He even started a hero.

MATTHEW LE TISSIER

(England, Attacking Midfielder)

There was one good reason why a club with limited resources like Southampton was able to stay in the

Premier League from its inception until 2005: Matthew Le Tissier. 'Le Tiss' played for the club from 1986 to 2002 and scored over 100 Premier League goals, the first player to do so who wasn't an out-and-out striker. Many of those goals were exquisite and delicate pieces of skill: a gem of a lob over Tim Flowers and a Sunday afternoon saunter through the Newcastle defence stand out in the mind.

Le Tissier had brilliant close control, good vision and a quite remarkable ability to strike the ball hard and true with little backlift. He wasn't the quickest but his touch was so instinctive that he stole a yard before the defender moved.

So why only eight caps for England? There were reservations about his work rate and his appetite; his loyalty to Southampton was perceived in some quarters as lack of ambition or fear of failure. The presence of Paul Gascoigne was another reason – the two players occupied the same space and, talented as he was, Le Tissier was not as good as Gascoigne. He lacked pace, so he couldn't be used further forward as he would never get away from international defenders.

Glenn Hoddle gave Le Tissier a trial for the 1998 World Cup squad in a 'B' match against Russia. Le Tissier responded with a hat-trick but Hoddle didn't pick him – and he didn't take Gascoigne either. Would it have been too big a gamble to leave out one of the squad makeweights like Rob Lee or Les Ferdinand and take a match-winner? Maybe. Maybe Le Tissier's failure at international level was just one of those quirks. But it's hard to believe he just wasn't good enough, remembering some of those Southampton performances.

Le Tissier was a brilliant penalty taker – of forty-eight attempts forty-seven found the net, a record of which both Matt Le Tissier and former Nottingham Forest keeper Mark Crossley are very proud.

108   10

Rq

Riquelme

JUAN ROMÁN RIQUELME

(Argentina, Playmaker)

Every nation has players who promise to be the answer to their footballing prayers: players with all the skills necessary to achieve everything the game can offer but never quite realise it. I'm not talking about boy wonders who never quite happen or players who get over-hyped and turn out just not to be that good, but really, really good top-class players who just miss out, for whatever reason.

England had Hoddle; France had Cantona; Germany had Schuster and Effenberg; and Argentina had Juan Román Riquelme.

Riquelme wasn't everyone's cup of tea. Barcelona signed him in 2002 against van Gaal's wishes and the Dutchman virtually ignored him (he should have played under Cruyff: Cruyff would have loved him). Riquelme moved to Villareal, where he became a cult hero as the club over-achieved outrageously, reaching the last four of the Champions League. Riquelme was playing his way, at the hub of the team where his vision and his balletic movement could have the maximum influence. He had time on the ball, time he created with use of space and vision. For a brief while he looked the unique talent first seen at Boca Juniors.

During this happy spell he played at the 2006 World Cup, masterminding a couple of scintillating Argentinian displays before the team lost to Germany on penalties. Two years later Riquelme captained his country as an over-age player as they won the Olympic football tournament in Beijing.

It couldn't last. Riquelme was soon at odds again, first with Manuel Pellegrini, his fellow countryman and Villareal manager, and later, inevitably, with Diego Maradona, now inexplicably *in situ* as Argentina coach. Riquelme retired in 2014, largely forgotten outside Argentina, Villareal and a few who remembered him destroy Serbia in 2006.

Riquelme admired the Brazilian playmaker Sócrates. He admired his worldview and his respect for the common people. He admired his belief that football is an art, and to achieve something beautiful is more important than simply to win a game. He might not hugely appreciate the scientific ordering in this book then...?

Index